CAMPAIGN 267

WILDERNESS AND SPOTSYLVANIA 1864

Grant versus Lee in the East

ANDY NUNEZ

ILLUSTRATED BY PETER DENNIS
Series editor Marcus Cowper

First published in Great Britain in 2014 by Osprey Publishing,
PO Box 883, Oxford, OX1 9PL, UK
PO Box 3985, New York, NY 10185-3985, USA
E-mail: info@ospreypublishing.com

ISBN: 978 1 4728 0147 0
E-book ISBN: 978 1 4728 0148 7
E-pub ISBN: 978 1 4728 0149 4

Editorial by Ilios Publishing Ltd, Oxford, UK (www.iliospublishing.com)
Index by Sandra Shotter
Typeset in Myriad Pro and Sabon
Maps by Bounford.com
3D bird's-eye view by The Black Spot
Battlescene illustrations by Peter Dennis
Originated by PDQ Media, Bungay, UK
Printed in China through Worldprint Ltd.

14 15 16 17 18   10 9 8 7 6 5 4 3 2 1

DEDICATION

Dedicated to my daughter Sarah, who looked at my library and said, "Dad, why don't you write a book about the Civil War?", and to the rest of my band of happy troops, David, Jason, Jonathan and their families, and my wife Nancy, without whom I would be an unhappy man.

ACKNOWLEDGMENTS

Special appreciation to my good friends Rich Allen and John Gilmer, the former being my driving partner and the latter making sure I got the history right. Also, the dedicated staff at the National Park Service are to be singled out for cheerfully answering my questions. This book would be the less without them. And last of all, my thanks to Peter Dennis, who turned my scribblings into beautiful paintings, and Marcus Cowper, my long-suffering editor.

ARTIST'S NOTE

Readers may care to note that the original paintings from which the color plates in this book were prepared are available for private sale. The Publishers retain all reproduction copyright whatsoever. All enquiries should be addressed to:

Peter Dennis, Fieldhead, The Park, Mansfield, Notts, NG18 2AT, UK
E-mail: magie.h@ntlworld.com

The Publishers regret that they can enter into no correspondence upon this matter.

THE WOODLAND TRUST

Osprey Publishing are supporting the Woodland Trust, the UK's leading woodland conservation charity, by funding the dedication of trees.

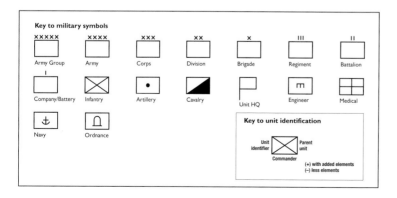

Key to military symbols

xxxxx Army Group	xxxx Army	xxx Corps	xx Division	x Brigade	III Regiment	II Battalion
I Company/Battery	Infantry	Artillery	Cavalry	Unit HQ	Engineer	Medical
Navy	Ordnance					

Key to unit identification

Unit identifier — Parent unit — Commander
(+) with added elements
(–) less elements

CONTENTS

Prelude to the Wilderness

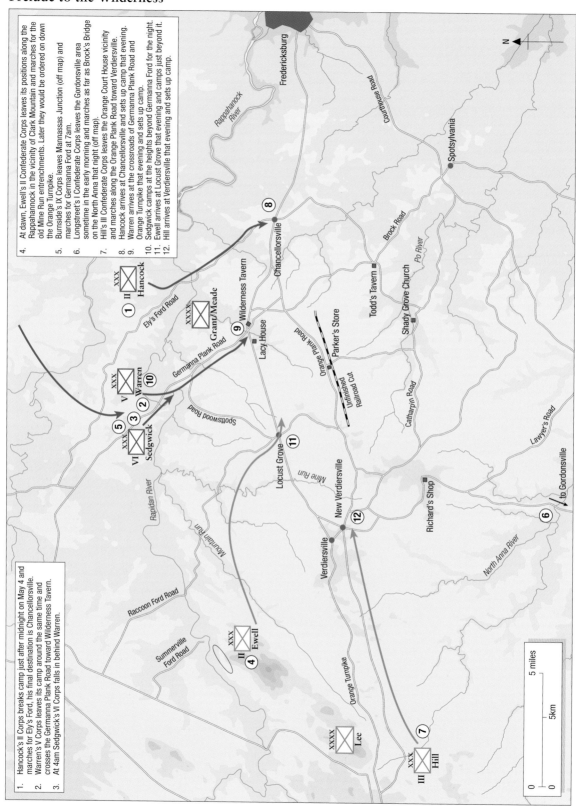

1. Hancock's II Corps breaks camp just after midnight on May 4 and marches for Ely's Ford, his final destination is Chancellorsville.
2. Warren's V Corps leaves its camp around the same time and crosses the Germanna Plank Road toward Wilderness Tavern.
3. At 4am Sedgwick's VI Corps falls in behind Warren.
4. At dawn, Ewell's II Confederate Corps leaves its positions along the Rappahannock in the vicinity of Clark Mountain and marches for the old Mine Run entrenchments. Later they would be ordered on down the Orange Turnpike.
5. Burnside's IX Corps leaves Mannassas Junction (off map) and marches for Germanna Ford at 7am.
6. Longstreet's I Confederate Corps leaves the Gordonsville area sometime in the early morning and marches as far as Brock's Bridge on the North Anna that night (off map).
7. Hill's III Confederate Corps leaves the Orange Court House vicinity and marches along the Orange Plank Road toward Verdiersville.
8. Hancock arrives at Chancellorsville and sets up camp that evening.
9. Warren arrives at the crossroads of Germanna Plank Road and Orange Turnpike that evening and sets up camp.
10. Sedgwick camps at the heights beyond Germanna Ford for the night.
11. Ewell arrives at Locust Grove that evening and camps just beyond it.
12. Hill arrives at Verdiersville that evening and sets up camp.

up troubled sectors. Masterful in defense, he was shakier in offense, gaining criticism for his lackluster pursuit of Lee and bad handling of the Mine Run campaign. He and Grant got along well enough, but once Grant arrived on the scene, Meade was unable to gain any favorable press and remained in Grant's shadow until the end of the war.

Winfield Scott Hancock (II Corps). "Hancock the Superb," named for Winfield Scott, one of the great commanders of the post-Revolutionary period, graduated from West Point in 1844. From there he rose from the quartermaster's department to a combat command during the Peninsula Campaign. Rising through the ranks as a volunteer, Hancock's units were always in the thick of action, whether at Antietam, Fredericksburg, Chancellorsville or Gettysburg, where he ended up commanding an entire wing of Meade's army and holding the center of the Union line until wounded. Recovering, he was back for the start of Grant's campaign against Lee. He was renowned for clear thinking, aggressive action and a cool head. He could rightly be called the best corps commander in the Union Army.

Ambrose Everett Burnside (IX Corps). An 1847 West Point graduate, Burnside left the Army in 1853 to manufacture a carbine of his own design. A failure at this, he raised his own regiment in Rhode Island at the start of the Civil War and advanced steadily after some successes in North Carolina until he reluctantly became head of the Army of the Potomac after McClellan was removed. Utterly defeated by Lee at Fredericksburg, he was replaced and headed the Department of the Ohio until he was reassigned to lead IX Corps under Grant directly, since Meade was technically his junior. This command structure would have its drawbacks.

John Sedgwick (V Corps). Initially in the cavalry, this 1837 West Point graduate, "Uncle John" Sedgwick fought in the Mexican War, the Seminole War and "Bleeding Kansas." He fought hard and well, rising to division command before the end of 1861. Wounded several times, he was an excellent corps commander and was loved by his men. Along with Hancock, he would be noted for solid, aggressive action going into the Wilderness.

ABOVE
George Meade, the victor of Gettysburg, had been unable to crush Lee in a stalemate lasting nearly a year. He was forced to accept Grant as his superior in an odd command arrangement. (Library of Congress)

LEFT
Winfield Hancock was a solid, aggressive leader who was eager to come to grips with the enemy after being wounded at Gettysburg. His skills would be sorely tested in the coming days. (Library of Congress)

Gouverneur Kemble Warren (VI Corps). Second in his class at West Point, this 1850 graduate was an expert topographical engineer and worked on several public works projects, as well as teaching mathematics at his alma mater. He was soon needed as an infantry officer once the war started and earned the title "Savior of Little Round Top" for his actions at this important part of the Union flank at Gettysburg. He substituted for Hancock as a corps commander when the latter was wounded, and his record was uneven. He displayed a penchant for taking unilateral actions that would come to haunt him during the Overland Campaign.

Philip Sheridan (Cavalry Corps). The only slow thing about Phil Sheridan was how long it took him to graduate from West Point in 1853 (five years). By the middle of 1862 he was commanding an infantry division and promoted to major-general by the end of that same year. Serving in the Midwest, he distinguished himself as a ferocious and agile commander. When Grant came east, he brought the feisty Sheridan with him to command the cavalry of the Army of the Potomac. The temperamental general of Irish descent rubbed several Eastern generals the wrong way, but he had Grant's confidence.

THE CONFEDERATE STATES OF AMERICA

Robert Edward Lee (Commander of the Army of Northern Virginia). "The Gray Fox," as he was known to his enemies, was the son of American Revolutionary War general Henry "Lighthorse Harry" Lee. He graduated second in the West Point class of 1829. He served in the engineer corps with distinction and was part of Winfield Scott's staff during the Mexican War. Afterward he served in Texas in the cavalry until his native Virginia seceded. His early war career as a brigadier-general was undistinguished and he was called "Granny Lee" and the "King of Spades." After becoming an advisor to Confederate President Jefferson Davis, he was given command of the Army of Northern Virginia when Joseph Johnston was wounded during the battles of the Seven Days. He held off or defeated nearly every Union general he faced. Blocked twice during incursions to the North, Lee stalemated Meade after retreating from Gettysburg during the fall and winter of 1863. As the weather warmed in 1864, he again waited for an opportunity to attack his Northern foe.

James Longstreet (I Corps). This native of South Carolina graduated from West Point in 1842. He fought in the Mexican War and was wounded at the battle of Chapultepec. Leaving the Army with the rank of major in June 1861, his rank rose steadily and he gained a reputation as a stable, if not overly aggressive, subordinate. He fought in every major battle in the Eastern Theater, from Bull Run to Appomattox, ending the war a lieutenant-general. His corps was temporarily detached to Tennessee where he was key to defeating the Union forces at Chickamauga in September 1863. Returning to Lee, he was barely able to get his forces into position during the battle of the Wilderness due to the distance he traveled.

Richard S. Ewell (II Corps). "Baldy" Ewell, an 1840 West Pointer, spent the two decades after his graduation as a company commander in the US Army. His reliance on specific orders from above brought the Confederacy to grief at Gettysburg and afterward. Ewell was trained to follow orders to the letter and when they were vague, he had little initiative. He lost his leg at Groveton during Second Manassas but was back by May 1863 and won handily at Second Winchester, but at Gettysburg, his desire for exact orders caused him to miss opportunities that cost Lee dearly when he failed to take the initiative. During his convalescence, he got married and some said it hurt his command ability.

Ambrose Powell Hill (III Corps), or A. P. Hill as he is usually known, was a man of great physical endurance, and expected the same from his men. Easily spotted in his red shirt, the 1847 West Point graduate resigned from the Army in 1861 and joined the Southern cause, rising from a colonelcy to command of III Corps following the death of Stonewall Jackson. Due to an unknown illness, his performance at Gettysburg was sub-par, giving Lee concerns about Hill's ability in the coming battle.

James Ewell Brown Stuart (Cavalry Corps). Thirteenth in his class at the US Military Academy, J. E. B. "Jeb" Stuart always served in mounted units. He rapidly rose to first lieutenant, stationed at Leavenworth, Kansas. He resigned his commission upon learning of Virginia's secession and was made colonel of the 1st Virginia Cavalry in time for First Manassas. His ability to gain information through reconnaissance and outposts gained the attention of Joseph E. Johnston who had him promoted to brigadier. His fame soared after coming under command of Lee during the battles of the Seven Days. Riding around the Union Army, he humiliated McClellan, then did it again to John Pope, even stealing Pope's uniform during Second Manassas. His artillery was key to battles at Antietam and Fredericksburg and he took over for the wounded Stonewall Jackson at Chancellorsville. He became too independent during the Gettysburg Campaign and improving Union cavalry embarrassed him at Brandy Station, then fought him to a standstill at Gettysburg, costing Lee the battle by raiding instead of providing critical information. By 1864, Major-General Stuart commanded two cavalry divisions, but his days of riding around the Union Army with impunity were long past.

John Brown Gordon was a businessman before the war and raised his own unit when it broke out. Rangy and bitter, he was an implacable foe, quickly rising through the ranks until he commanded a Georgia brigade at the start of the Wilderness campaign. He was wounded at Antietam, but recovered in time for Chancellorsville. He was a natural leader with a good eye for terrain and was always ready to take the fight to the enemy, traits which would make his reputation in the coming battles.

Robert E. Lee, son of a Revolutionary War hero, bested Union generals over several campaigns. He seemed invincible fighting on his native Virginia soil, but this was the first time he was to tackle Grant. (Library of Congress)

OPPOSING ARMIES

THE UNION ARMY

The Union Army of the Potomac at the start of the Wilderness Campaign was large and well equipped. Lieutenant-General Grant could count on roughly 102,000 men, not counting the 19,000 men of IX Corps and the 36,956 men of the Army of the James. All told, he had 159,075 men that he could throw at Lee and Richmond. As we shall see, he had a plan that would use them more effectively than past commanders.

While impressive on paper, there was more to the Army of the Potomac than meets the eye. Popular history assumes that Grant came in and turned Meade's army into a superior fighting force, but this glosses over the hard work Meade did to reorganize his army with an eye to making it more efficient to command against an opponent who could strike hard and fast. Meade came up with a good plan to flank Lee at Mine Run, but his army wasn't able to move fast enough to execute the maneuver and Lee was able to form a tough defensive line. Meade did the right thing by backing off, but paid for it politically.

Seeing his army was unable to move as he desired, Meade decided to simplify its structure. He knew that he had three good corps commanders: Hancock, Sedgwick, and Warren; though the latter was a bit odd at times, but his performance at Gettysburg was solid. Meade decided to dissolve I and III Corps and redistribute their divisions among these three leaders. The largest corps became Hancock's II Corps, but he was able to handle it easily enough. The former I and III Corps units were a bit let down.

Grant's arrival took things further. Grant found much to like about the Army of the Potomac. The men were well supplied and well fed. Morale among the veteran troops was good, but many of them were mustering out as their enlistments ended. There were plenty of

Gouverneur Warren held his ground at Gettysburg. He had his own ideas and this campaign would test his resolve. (Library of Congress)

conscripts mustering in, and they were being trained hard, but unlike the Confederate practice of mixing new recruits into veteran units, the Union Army had a penchant for creating entirely new regiments. These green regiments, no matter how much they drilled, were not previously exposed to combat and their reliability was in question.

Grant and Meade got along, but the arrival of Phil Sheridan caused some friction because he had his own ideas on how to use the Union cavalry. Instead of picket duty and supply line protection, Sheridan, with Grant's approval, wanted the cavalry as a long-range strike force, much the same way that Rebel cavalry was used. Sheridan got his way and set about reorganizing the cavalry corps. He sacked several officers and placed infantry officers in charge of two divisions. Though still hampered by Meade's insistence on some of the cavalry acting as a flanking screen to guard the supply wagons, Sheridan got his way and Union cavalry would play its part in the upcoming campaign.

The Union artillery was in the capable hands of Henry J. Hunt, a brigadier of volunteers who had uneven relationships with his superiors. McClellan liked him, Hooker did not. His artillery proved devastating at Gettysburg, but he and Meade did not see eye to eye. Grant recognized the man's genius for the placement and massing of batteries both in offense and defense; though Hunt's magnificent guns would play no decisive role in the dense woods of the Wilderness.

Supply for the Union Army was typical of its day, tied to roads and railroads, making any advance ponderous due to its reliance on a secure line. Union factories were churning out food, clothing, weapons, and equipment. Through all the leadership changes, Rufus Ingalls remained the chief quartermaster of the Army of the Potomac for the entire war, with 4,300 wagons backing up the Army along with tens of thousands of mules. It was estimated by Ingalls that if he strung all his wagons out in a line they would stretch from the Rapidan River to Richmond. Grant had put him in charge of supplying not just the Army of the Potomac, but all forces operating in the Virginia theater, tasking him to set up "flying depots" at critical spots. The men were to be cut loose from the supply routes, each soldier carrying 50 rounds of ammunition and three days' rations.

Philip Sheridan (left) was originally an infantry general, but Grant put him in charge of the Army of the Potomac's cavalry. Sheridan was a fighter, both against the enemy and his own peers at times. (Library of Congress)

13

UNION ORDER OF BATTLE

Lt. Gen. Ulysses S. Grant

Army of the Potomac	Maj. Gen. George G. Meade,
Provost Guard	Brig. Gen. Marsena R. Patrick
1st Massachusetts Cavalry, Companies C And D	
	Capt. Edward A. Flint
80th New York Infantry (20th Militia)	Col. Theodore B. Gates
3rd Pennsylvania Cavalry	Maj. James W. Walsh
68th Pennsylvania Infantry	Lt. Col. Robert E. Winslow
114th Pennsylvania Infantry	Col. Charles H. T. Collis
Volunteer Engineer Brigade	Brig. Gen. Henry W. Benham
15th New York Engineers	Maj. William A. Ketchum
50th New York Engineers	Lt. Col. Ira Spaulding
Battalion US Engineers	Capt. George H. Mendell
Guards and Orderlies	
Independent Company Oneida (New York) Cavalry	
	Capt. Daniel P. Mann

II CORPS — MAJ. GEN. WINFIELD S. HANCOCK

Escort

1st Vermont Cavalry, Company M	Capt. John H. Hazelton

1st Division — Brig. Gen. Francis C. Barlow

1st Brigade	Col. Nelson A. Miles
26th Michigan	Maj. Lemuel Saviers
61st New York	Lt. Col. K. Oscar Broady
81st Pennsylvania	Col. H. Boyd McKeen
140th Pennsylvania	Col. John Fraser
183rd Pennsylvania	Col. George P. McLean
2nd Brigade	Col. Thomas A. Smyth
28th Massachusetts	Lt. Col. George W. Cartwright
63rd New York	Maj. Thomas Touhy
69th New York	Capt. Richard Moroney
88th New York	Capt. Denis F. Burke
116th Pennsylvania	Lt. Col. Richard C. Dale
3rd Brigade	Col. Paul Frank
39th New York	Col. Augustus Funk
52nd New York	Maj. Henry M. Karples
57th New York	Lt. Col. Alford B. Chapman
111th New York	Capt. Aaron P. Seeley
125th New York	Lt. Col. Aaron B. Myer
126th New York	Capt. Winfield Scott
4th Brigade	Col. John R. Brooke
2nd Delaware	Col. William P. Baily
64th New York	Maj. Leman W. Bradley
66th New York	Lt. Col. John S. Haremell
53rd Pennsylvania	Lt. Col. Richards McMichael
145th Pennsylvania	Col. Hiram L. Brown
148th Pennsylvania	Col. James A. Beaver

2nd Division — Brig. Gen. John Gibbon

Provost Guard	
2nd Company Minnesota Sharpshooters	
	Capt. Mahlon Black
1st Brigade	Brig. Gen. Alexander S. Webb
19th Maine	Col. Selden Connor
1st Company Andrew (Massachusetts) Sharpshooters	
	Lt. Samuel G. Gilbreth
15th Massachusetts	Maj. I. Harris Hooper
19th Massachusetts	Maj. Edmund Rice
20th Massachusetts	Maj. Henry L. Abbott
7th Michigan	Maj. Sylvanus W. Curtis
42nd New York	Maj. Patrick J. Downing
59th New York	Capt. William McFadden
82nd New York (2nd Militia)	Col. Henry W. Hudson
2nd Brigade	Brig. Gen. Joshua T. Owen
152nd New York	Lt. Col. George W. Thompson
69th Pennsylvania	Maj. William Davis
71st Pennsylvania	Lt. Col. Charles Kochersperger
72nd Pennsylvania	Col. DeWitt C. Baxter
106th Pennsylvania	Capt. Robert H. Ford
3rd Brigade	Col. Samuel S. Carroll
14th Connecticut	Col. Theodore G. Ellis
1st Delaware	Lt. Col. Daniel Woodall
14th Indiana	Col. John Coons
12th New Jersey	Lt. Col. Thomas H. Davis
10th New York Battalion	Capt. George M. Dewey
108th New York	Col. Charles J. Powers
4th Ohio	Lt. Col. Leonard W. Carpenter
8th Ohio	Lt. Col. Franklin Sawyer
7th West Virginia	Lt. Col. Jonathan H. Lockwood

3rd Division — Maj. Gen. David B. Birney

1st Brigade	Brig. Gen. J. H. Hobart Ward
20th Indiana	Col. William C. L. Taylor
3rd Maine	Col. Moses B. Lakeman
40th New York	Col. Thomas W. Egan
86th New York	Lt. Col. Jacob H. Lansing
124th New York	Col. Francis M. Cummins
99th Pennsylvania	Lt. Col. Edwin R. Biles
110th Pennsylvania	Lt. Col. Isaac Rogers
141st Pennsylvania	Lt. Col. Guy H. Watkins
2nd US Sharpshooters	Lt. Col. Homer R. Stoughton
2nd Brigade	Brig. Gen. Alexander Hays
4th Maine	Col. Elijah Walker
17th Maine	Col. George W. West
3rd Michigan	Col. Byron R. Pierce
5th Michigan	Lt. Col. John Pulford
93rd New York	Maj. Samuel McConihe
57th Pennsylvania	Col. Peter Sides
63rd Pennsylvania	Lt. Col. John A. Danks
105th Pennsylvania	Col. Calvin A. Craig
1st US Sharpshooters	Maj. Charles P. Mattocks

4th Division	**Brig. Gen. Gershom Mott**
1st Brigade	Col. Robert McAllister
1st Massachusetts	Col. Napoleon B. McLaughlen
16th Massachusetts	Lt. Col. Waldo Merriam
5th New Jersey	Col. William J. Sewell
6th New Jersey	Lt. Col. Stephen R. Gilkyson
7th New Jersey	Maj. Frederick Cooper
8th New Jersey	Col. John Ramsey
11th New Jersey	Lt. Col. John Schoonover
26th Pennsylvania	Maj. Samuel G. Moffett
115th Pennsylvania	Maj. William A. Reilly
2nd Brigade	Col. William R. Brewster
11th Massachusetts	Col. William Blaisdell
70th New York	Capt. William H. Hugo
71st New York	Lt. Col. Thomas Rafferty
72nd New York	Lt. Col. John Leonard
73rd New York	Lt. Col. Michael W. Burns
74th New York	Col. Thomas Holt
120th New York	Capt. Abram L. Lockwood
84th Pennsylvania	Lt. Col. Milton Opp
Artillery Brigade	Col. John C. Tidball
Maine Light, 6th Battery (F)	Capt. Edwin B. Dow
Massachusetts Light, 10th Battery	Capt. J. Henry Sleeper
New Hampshire Light, 1st Battery	Capt. Frederick M. Edgell
1st New York Light, Battery G	Capt. Nelson Ames
4th New York Heavy, 3rd Battalion	Lt. Col. Thomas Allcock
1st Pennsylvania Light, Battery F	Capt. R. Bruce Ricketts
1st Rhode Island Light, Battery A	Capt. William A. Arnold
1st Rhode Island Light, Battery B	Capt. T. Frederick Brown
4th United States, Battery K	Lt. John W. Roder
5th United States, Batteries C and I	Lt. James Gilliss

V CORPS	**MAJ. GEN. GOUVERNEUR K. WARREN**
Provost Guard	
12th New York Battalion	Maj. Henry W. Rider
1st Division	**Brig. Gen. Charles Griffin**
1st Brigade	Brig. Gen. Romeyn B. Ayres
140th New York	Col. George Ryan
146th New York	Col. David T. Jenkins
91st Pennsylvania	Lt. Col. Joseph H. Sinex
155th Pennsylvania	Lt. Col. Alfred L. Pearson
2nd United States, Companies B, C, F, H, I, and K	
	Capt. James W. Long
11th United States, Companies B, C, D, E, F, and G,	
1st Battalion	Capt. Francis M. Cooley
12th United States, Companies A, B, C, D, and G,	
1st Battalion	Maj. Luther B. Bruen
12th United States, Companies A, C, D, F, and H,	
2nd Battalion	
14th United States,	
1st Battalion	Capt. Edward Mck. Hudson
17th United States, Companies A, C, D, G, and H,	

1st Battalion	Capt. James F. Grimes
17th United States, Companies A, B, and C, 2nd Battalion	
2nd Brigade	Col. Jacob B. Sweitzer
9th Massachusetts	Col. Patrick R. Guiney
22nd Massachusetts	Col. William S. Tilton
32nd Massachusetts	Col. George L. Prescott
4th Michigan	Lt. Col. George W. Lurebard
62nd Pennsylvania	Lt. Col. James C. Hull
3rd Brigade	Brig. Gen. Joseph J. Bartlett
20th Maine	Maj. Ellis Spear
18th Massachusetts	Col. Joseph Hayes
1st Michigan	Lt. Col. William A. Throop
16th Michigan	Maj. Robert T. Elliott
44th New York	Lt. Col. Freeman Conner
83rd Pennsylvania	Col. Orpheus S. Woodward
118th Pennsylvania	Col. James Gwyn
2nd Division	**Brig. Gen. John C. Robinson**
1st Brigade	Col. Samuel H. Leonard
16th Maine	Col. Charles W. Tilden
13th Massachusetts	Capt. Charles H. Hovey
89th Massachusetts	Col. Phineas S. Davis
104th New York	Col. Gilbert G. Prey
2nd Brigade	Brig. Gen. Henry Baxter
12th Massachusetts	Col. James L. Bates
83rd New York (9th Militia)	Col. Joseph A. Moesch
97th New York	Col. Charles Wheelock
11th Pennsylvania	Col. Richard Coulter
88th Pennsylvania	Capt. George B. Rhoads
90th Pennsylvania	Col. Peter Lyle
3rd Brigade	Col. Andrew W. Denison
1st Maryland	Maj. Benjamin H. Schley
4th Maryland	Col. Richard N. Bowerman
7th Maryland	Col. Charles E. Phelps
8th Maryland	Lt. Col. John G. Johannes
3rd Division	**Brig. Gen. Samuel W. Crawford**
1st Brigade	Col. William McCandless
1st Pennsylvania Reserves	Col. William C. Talley
2nd Pennsylvania Reserves	Lt. Col. Patrick McDonough
6th Pennsylvania Reserves	Col. Wellington H. Ent
7th Pennsylvania Reserves	Maj. LeGrand B. Speece
11th Pennsylvania Reserves	Col. Samuel M. Jackson
13th Pennsylvania Reserves (1st Rifles)	Maj. William R. Hartshorne
3rd Brigade	Col. Joseph W. Fisher
5th Pennsylvania Reserves	Lt. Col. George Dare
8th Pennsylvania Reserves	Col. Silas M. Baily
10th Pennsylvania Reserves	Lt. Col. Ira Ayer, Jr
12th Pennsylvania Reserves	Lt. Col. Richard Gustin
4th Division	**Brig. Gen. James S. Wadsworth**
1st Brigade	Brig. Gen. Lysander Cutler
7th Indiana	Col. Ira G. Grover
19th Indiana	Col. Samuel J. Williams

24th Michigan	Col. Henry A. Morrow
1st New York Battalion Sharpshooters	Capt. Volney J. Shipman
2nd Wisconsin	Lt. Col. John Mansfield
6th Wisconsin	Col. Edward S. Bragg
7th Wisconsin	Col. William W. Robinson
2nd Brigade	Brig. Gen. James C. Rice
76th New York	Lt. Col. John E. Cook
84th New York (14th Militia)	Col. Edward B. Fowler
95th New York	Col. Edward Pye
147th New York	Col. Francis C. Miller
56th Pennsylvania	Col. J. William Holmann
3rd Brigade	Col. Roy Stone
121st Pennsylvania	Capt. Samuel T. Lloyd
142nd Pennsy1vania	Maj. Horatio N. Warren
143rd Pennsy1vania	Col. Edmund L. Dana
149th Pennsy1vania	Lt. Col. John Irvin
150th Pennsylvania	Capt. George W. Jones
Artillery Brigade	Col. Charles S. Wainwright
Massachusetts Light, Battery C	Capt. Augustus P. Martin
Massachusetts Light, Battery E	Capt. Charles A. Phillips
1st New York Light, Battery D	Capt. George B. Winslow
1st New York Light, Batteries E and L	Lt. George Breck
1st New York Light, Battery H	Capt. Charles E. Mink
4th New York Heavy, 2nd Battalion	Maj. William Arthur
1st Pennsylvania Light, Battery B	Capt. James H. Cooper
4th United States, Battery B	Lt. James Stewart
5th United States, Battery D	Lt. Benjamin F. Rittenhouse
Heavy Artillery Brigade	Col. J. Howard Kitching
6th New York	
15th New York (1st and 3rd Batteries)	

VI CORPS   MAJ. GEN. JOHN SEDGWICK (KILLED MAY 9 AND REPLACED BY HORATIO WRIGHT)

Escort

8th Pennsylvania Cavalry, Company A	Capt. Charles E. Fellows

1st Division	**Brig. Gen. Horatio G. Wright**
1st Brigade	Col. Henry W. Brown
1st New Jersey	Lt. Col. William Henry, Jr
2nd New Jersey	Lt. Col. Charles Wiebecke
3rd New Jersey	Capt. Samuel T. Dubois
4th New Jersey	Lt. Col. Charles Ewing
10th New Jersey	Col. Henry O. Ryerson
15th New Jersey	Col. William H. Penrose
2nd Brigade	Col. Emory Upton
5th Maine	Col. Clark S. Edwards
121st New York	Lt. Col. Egbert Olcott
95th Pennsylvania	Lt. Col. Edward Carroll
96th Pennsylvania	Lt. Col. William H. Lessig
3rd Brigade	Brig. Gen. David A. Russell
6th Maine	Maj. George Fuller

49th Pennsylvania	Col. Thomas Hulings
119th Pennsylvania	Maj. Henry P. Truefitt, Jr
5th Wisconsin	Lt. Col. Theodore B. Catlin
4th Brigade	Brig. Gen. Alexander Shaler
65th New York	Col. Joseph E. Hamblin
67th New York	Col. Nelson Cross
122nd New York	Lt. Col. Augustus W. Dwight
82nd Pennsylvania (Detachment)	

2nd Division	**Brig. Gen. George W. Getty**
1st Brigade	Brig. Gen. Frank Wheaton
62nd New York	Col. David J. Nevin
93rd Pennsylvania	Lt. Col. John S. Long
98th Pennsylvania	Col. John F. Ballier
102nd Pennsylvania	Col. John W. Patterson
139th Pennsylvania	Lt. Col. William H. Moody
2nd Brigade	Col. Lewis A. Grant
2nd Vermont	Col. Newton Stone
3rd Vermont	Col. Thomas O. Seaver
4th Vermont	Col. George P. Foster
5th Vermont	Lt. Col. John R. Lewis
6th Vermont	Col. Elisha L. Barney
3rd Brigade	Brig. Gen. Thomas H. Neill
7th Maine	Col. Edwin C. Mason
43rd New York	Lt. Col. John Wilson
49th New York	Col. Daniel D. Bidwell
77th New York	Maj. Nathan S. Babcock
61st Pennsylvania	Col. George F. Smith
4th Brigade	Brig. Gen. Henry L. Eustis
7th Massachusetts	Col. Thomas D. Johns
10th Massachusetts	Lt. Col. Joseph B. Parsons
37th Massachusetts	Col. Oliver Edwards
2nd Rhode Island	Lt. Col. Samuel B. M. Read

3rd Division	**Brig. Gen. James B. Ricketts**
1st Brigade	Brig. Gen. William H. Morris
14th New Jersey	Lt. Col. Caldwell K. Hall
106th New York	Lt. Col. Charles Townsend
151st New York	Lt. Col. Thomas M. Fay
87th Pennsylvania	Col. John W. Schall
10th Vermont	Lt. Col. William W. Henry
2nd Brigade	Brig. Gen. Truman Seymour
6th Maryland	Col. John W. Horn
110th Ohio	Col. J. Warren Keifer
122nd Ohio	Col. William H. Ball
126th Ohio	Col. Benjamin F. Smith
67th Pennsylvania (Detachment)	Capt. George W. Guss
138th Pennsylvania	Col. Matthew R. McClennan
Artillery Brigade	Col. Charles H. Tompkins
Maine Light, 4th Battery (D)	Lt. Melville C. Kimball
Massachusetts Light, 1st Battery (A)	Capt. William H. McCartney
New York Light, 1st Battery	Capt. Andrew Cowan
New York Light, 3rd Battery	Capt. William A. Harn

4th New York Heavy, 1st Battalion	Maj. Thomas D. Sears
1st Rhode Island Light, Battery C	Capt. Richard Waterman
1st Rhode Island Light, Battery E	Capt. William B. Rhodes
1st Rhode Island Light, Battery G	Capt. George W. Adams
5th United States, Battery M	Capt. James McKnight

IX CORPS — MAJ. GEN. AMBROSE E. BURNSIDE

Provost Guard
| 8th US Infantry | Capt. Milton Cogswell |

1st Division — **Brig. Gen. Thomas G. Stevenson**
1st Brigade	Col. Sumner Carruth
35th Massachusetts	Maj. Nathaniel Wales
56th Massachusetts	Col. Charles E. Griswold
57th Massachusetts	Col. William F. Bartlett
59th Massachusetts	Col. J. Parker Gould
4th United States	Capt. Charles H. Brightly
10th United States	Maj. Samuel B. Hayman
2nd Brigade	Col. Daniel Leasure
3rd Maryland	Col. Joseph M. Sudsburg
21st Massachusetts	Lt. Col. George P. Hawkes
100th Pennsylvania	Lt. Col. Matthew M. Dawson
Artillery	
Maine Light, 2nd Battery (B)	Capt. Albert F. Thomas
Massachusetts Light, 14th Battery	Capt. Joseph W. B. Wright

2nd Division — **Brig. Gen. Robert B. Potter**
1st Brigade	Col. Zenas R. Bliss
36th Massachusetts	Maj. William F. Draper
58th Massachusetts	Lt. Col. John C. Whiton
51st New York	Col. Charles W. LeGendre
45th Pennsylvania	Col. John I. Curtin
48th Pennsylvania	Lt. Col. Henry Pleasants
7th Rhode Island	Capt. Theodore Winn
2nd Brigade	Col. Simon G. Griffin
31st Maine	Lt. Col. Thomas Hight
82nd Maine	Maj. Arthur Deering
6th New Hampshire	Lt. Col. Henry H. Pearson
9th New Hampshire	Lt. Col. John W. Babbitt
11th New Hampshire	Col. Walter Harriman
17th Vermont	Lt. Col. Charles Cummings
Artillery	
Massachusetts Light, 11th Battery	Capt. Edward J. Jones
New York Light, 19th Battery	Capt. Edward W. Rogers

3rd Division — **Brig. Gen. Orlando B. Willcox**
1st Brigade	Col. John F. Hartranft
2nd Michigan	Col. William Humphrey
8th Michigan	Col. Frank Graves
17th Michigan	Col. Constant Luce
27th Michigan	Maj. Samuel Moody
109th New York	Col. Benjamin F. Tracy
51st Pennsylvania	Lt. Col. Edwin Schall
2nd Brigade	Col. Benjamin C. Christ
1st Michigan Sharpshooters	Col. Charles V. De Land
20th Michigan	Lt. Col. Byron M. Cutcheon
70th New York	Col. David Morrison
60th Ohio	Lt. Col. James N. McElroy
50th Pennsylvania	Lt. Col. Edward Overton, Jr
Artillery	
Maine Light, 7th Battery (G)	Capt. Adelbert B. Twitchell
New York Light, 34th Battery	Capt. Jacob Roemer

4th Division — **Brig. Gen. Edward Ferrero**
1st Brigade	Col. Joshua K. Sigfried
27th US Colored Troops	Lt. Col. Charles J. Wright
30th US Colored Troops	Col. Delavan Bates
39th US Colored Troops	Col. Ozora P. Stearns
43rd US Colored Troops	Lt. Col. H. Seymour Hall
2nd Brigade	Col. Henry G. Thomas
30th Connecticut (Colored) (Detachment)	Capt. Charles Robinson
19th US Colored Troops	Lt. Col. Joseph G. Perkins
23rd US Colored Troops	Lt. Col. Cleaveland J. Campbell
Artillery	
Pennsylvania Light, Battery D	Capt. George W. Durell
Vermont Light, 3rd Battery	Capt. Romeo H. Start
Cavalry	
3rd New Jersey	Col. Andrew J. Morrison
22nd New York	Col. Samuel J. Crooks
2nd Ohio	Lt. Col. George A. Purington
13th Pennsylvania	Maj. Michael Kerwin
Reserve Artillery	Capt. John Edwards, Jr
New York Light, 27th Battery	Capt. John B. Eaton
1st Rhode Island Light, Battery D	Capt. William W. Buckley
1st Rhode Island Light, Battery H	Capt. Crawford Allen, Jr
2nd United States, Battery E	Lt. James S. Dudley
3rd United States, Battery G	Lt. Edmund Pendleton
3rd United States, Batteries L and M	Lt. Erskine Gittings
Provisional Brigade	Col. Elisha G. Marshall
24th New York Cavalry (Dismounted)	Col. William C. Raulston
14th New York Heavy Artillery	Lt. Col. Clarence H. Corning
2nd Pennsylvania Provisional Heavy Artillery	Col. Thomas Wilhelm

CAVALRY CORPS — MAJ. GEN. PHILIP H. SHERIDAN

Escort
| 6th United States | Capt. Ira W. Claflin |

1st Division — **Brig. Gen. Alfred T. A. Torbert**
1st Brigade	Brig. Gen. George A. Custer
1st Michigan	Lt. Col. Peter Stagg
5th Michigan	Col. Russell A. Alger
6th Michigan	Maj. James H. Kidd
7th Michigan	Maj. Henry W. Granger
2nd Brigade	Col. Thomas C. Devin
4th New York	Lt. Col. William R. Parnell
6th New York	Lt. Col. William H. Crocker

9th New York	Col. William Sackett
17th Pennsylvania	Lt. Col. James Q. Anderson
Reserve Brigade	Brig. Gen. Wesley Merritt
19th New York (1st Dragoons)	Col. Alfred Gibbs
6th Pennsylvania	Maj. James Starr
1st United States	Capt. Nelson B. Sweitzer
2nd United States	Capt. Theophilus F. Rodenbough
5th United States	Capt. Abraham K. Arnold
2nd Division	**Brig. Gen. David Mcm. Gregg**
1st Brigade	Brig. Gen. Henry E. Davies, Jr
1st Massachusetts	Maj. Lucius M. Sargent
1st New Jersey	Lt. Col. John W. Kester
6th Ohio	Col. William Stedman
1st Pennsylvania	Col. John P. Taylor
2nd Brigade	Col. J. Irvin Gregg
1st Maine	Col. Charles H. Smith
10th New York	Maj. M. Henry Avery
2nd Pennsylvania	Lt. Col. Joseph P. Brinton
4th Pennsylvania	Lt. Col. George H. Covode
8th Pennsylvania	Lt. Col. Samuel Wilson
16th Pennsylvania	Lt. Col. John K. Robison
3rd Division	**Brig. Gen. James H. Wilson**
Escort	
8th Illinois (Detachment)	Lt. William W. Long
1st Brigade	Col. Timothy M. Bryan, Jr
1st Connecticut	Maj. Erastus Blakeslee
2nd New York	Col. Otto Harhaus
5th New York	Lt. Col. John Hammond
18th Pennsylvania	Lt. Col. William P. Brinton
2nd Brigade	Col. George H. Chapman
3rd Indiana	Maj. William Patton
8th New York	Lt. Col. William H. Benjamin
1st Vermont	Lt. Col. Addison W. Preston

ARTILLERY	**BRIG. GEN. HENRY J. HUNT**
Artillery Reserve	**Col. Henry S. Burton**
1st Brigade	Col. J. Howard Kitching
6th New York Heavy	Lt. Col. Edmund R. Travis
15th New York Heavy	Col. Louis Schirmer
2nd Brigade	Maj. John A. Tompkins
Maine Light, 5th Battery (E)	Capt. Greenleaf T. Stevens
1st New Jersey Light, Battery A	Capt. William Hexamer
1st New Jersey Light, Battery B	Capt. A. Judson Clark
New York Light, 5th Battery	Capt. Elijah D. Taft
New York Light, 12th Battery	Capt. George F. McKnight
1st New York Light, Battery B	Capt. Albert S. Sheldon
3rd Brigade	Maj. Robert H. Fitzhugh
Massachusetts Light, 9th Battery	Capt. John Bigelow
New York Light, 15th Battery	Capt. Patrick Hart
1st New York Light, Battery C	Lt. William H. Phillips
New York Light, 11th Battery	Capt. John E. Burton
1st Ohio Light, Battery H	Lt. William A. Ewing
5th United States, Battery E	Lt. John R. Brinckle
Horse Artillery	
1st Brigade	Capt. James M. Robertson
New York Light, 6th Battery	Capt. Joseph W. Martin
2nd United States, Batteries B and L	Lt. Edward Heaton
2nd United States, Battery D	Lt. Edward B. Williston
2nd United States, Battery M	Lt. Alexander C. M. Pennington, Jr
4th United States, Battery A	Lt. Rufus King, Jr
4th United States, Batteries C and E	Lt. Charles L. Fitzhugh
2nd Brigade	Capt. Dunbar R. Ransom
1st United States, Batteries E and G	Lt. Frank S. French
1st United States, Batteries H and I	Capt. Alanson M. Randol
1st United States, Battery K	Lt. John Egan
2nd United States, Battery A	Lt. Robert Clarke
2nd United States, Battery G	Lt. William N. Dennison
3rd United States, Batteries C, F, and K	Lt. James R. Kelly

THE CONFEDERATE ARMY

Robert E. Lee was able to use the long period of relative inaction between Gettysburg and the Wilderness to rebuild his Army of Northern Virginia to its pre-Gettysburg strength. Opposing Grant's forces were 85,540 men of the Department of Richmond and the Army of Northern Virginia. This large force, two-thirds the size of Grant's, was nowhere near what Lee could actually muster to meet the Union thrust. One of his divisions, that of George Pickett, was serving in North Carolina, and despite entreaties to Davis, would not join Lee for the events covered in this book.

The resulting casualties from Gettysburg and Mine Run had taken a toll on Lee's army, and the rigors of warfare had taken a toll on Lee, personally, along with his commanders. Inadequate food and a series of battles from Chancellorsville to Mine Run put Lee's health at risk, and he was ill several times during the ensuing months. Of his corps commanders, only Longstreet enjoyed good health. Ewell suffered from a missing leg, had recently wed and was still grappling with the challenge of taking over the late Thomas "Stonewall" Jackson's II Corps. Hill, a man who could be counted on to move men fast, was also battling some ailment that sapped his strength.

The Army of Northern Virginia as a fighting force was undersupplied and underfed. Despite poor conditions, their morale remained high and conscription actually increased after the beginning of 1864 from some 300 men per month to 600 men per month in the theater. It was Davis, not any other factor, that reduced Lee's total strength from nearly 79,000 to just under 60,000 at the start of the campaign. Worse for Lee, Longstreet's corps was not available on the first day of battle. Davis was concerned with possible Union seaborne invasions along the coast, or up the James River to Richmond. He also planned to try to clear the Carolinas of Union lodgments, but such plans failed, tying down more troops better used to battle Grant.

Jeb Stuart's cavalry corps was a corps in name only; it was originally little more than a division, and suffered the loss of Imboden's and Jenkins' brigades to operations in the Blue Ridge Mountains. The artillery corps had been depleted also, with units held back to Richmond, leaving Lee only 58 cannon available to his army. Much has been made of the failure of the Confederacy to understand the need for a reliable, cohesive rail service, but it was never the efficient transport arm the Union possessed. The Commissary Department was similarly hobbled by lack of rail transport, and Sherman's activities in Tennessee were depriving the Confederacy of more and more rolling stock all the time. Blockade runners could not hope to supply the troops with adequate weapons and there was a lack of shoes, tents and many other necessities that Grant enjoyed in abundance.

James Longstreet was one of Lee's best tacticians, but he was camped at some distance from the battleground and his absence on the first day would be sorely missed. (University of Kentucky)

Jeb Stuart was Lee's eyes and ears. When the flamboyant cavalry commander strayed at Gettysburg, many thought it cost him the battle. (Library of Congress)

CONFEDERATE ORDER OF BATTLE

Army Of Northern Virginia | General Robert E. Lee

I CORPS	LT. GEN. JAMES LONGSTREET
	(RICHARD H. ANDERSON AFTER MAY 6)

Kershaw's Division	Brig. Gen. Joseph B. Kershaw
Kershaw's Brigade	Col. John W. Henagan
2nd South Carolina	Lt. Col. Franklin Gaillard
3rd South Carolina	Col. James D. Nance
7th South Carolina	Capt. James Mitchell
8th South Carolina	Lt. Col. Eli T. Stackhouse
15th South Carolina	Col. John B. Davis
3rd South Carolina Battalion	Capt. B. M. Whitener
Wofford's Brigade	Brig. Gen. William T. Wofford
16th Georgia	
18th Georgia	
24th Georgia	
Cobb's (Georgia) Legion	
Phillips' (Georgia) Legion	
3rd Georgia Battalion Sharpshooters	
Humphreys' Brigade	Brig. Gen. Benjamin G. Humphreys
13th Mississippi	Maj. George L. Donald
17th Mississippi	
18th Mississippi	Capt. William H. Lewis
21st Mississippi	Col. D. N. Moody
Bryan's Brigade	Brig. Gen. Goode Bryan
10th Georgia	Col. Willis C. Holt
50th Georgia	Col. Peter McGlashan
51st Georgia	Col. Edward Ball
53rd Georgia	Col. James P. Simms

Field's Division	Maj. Gen. Charles W. Field
Jenkins' Brigade	Brig. Gen. Micah Jenkins
1st South Carolina	Col. James R. Hagood
2nd South Carolina (Rifles)	Col. Robert E. Bowen
5th South Carolina	Col. A. Coward
6th South Carolina	Col. John Bratton
Palmetto (South Carolina) Sharpshooters	
	Col. Joseph Walker
Law's Brigade	Brig. Gen. E. McIver Law
4th Alabama	Col. Pinckney D. Bowles
15th Alabama	
44th Alabama	Col. William F. Perry
47th Alabama	
48th Alabama	Lt. Col. William M. Hardwick
Anderson's Brigade	Brig. Gen. George T. Anderson
7th Georgia	
8th Georgia	
9th Georgia	
11th Georgia	
59th Georgia	Lt. Col. Bolivar H. Gee

Gregg's Brigade	Brig. Gen. John Gregg
3rd Arkansas	Col. Van H. Manning
1st Texas	
4th Texas	Col. John P. Bane
5th Texas	Lt. Col. King Bryan
Benning's Brigade	Brig. Gen. Henry L. Benning
2nd Georgia	
15th Georgia	Col. Dudley M. Du Bose
17th Georgia	
20th Georgia	

Artillery	Brig. Gen. E. Porter Alexander
Huger's Battalion	Lt. Col. Frank Huger
Fickling's (South Carolina) Battery	
Moody's (Louisiana) Battery	
Parker's (Virginia) Battery	
Smith's, J. D. (Virginia), Battery	
Taylor's (Virginia) Battery	
Woolfolk's (Virginia) Battery	
Haskell's Battalion	Maj. John C. Haskell
Flanner's (North Carolina) Battery	
Garden's (South Carolina) Battery	
Lamkin's (Virginia) Battery (Unequipped)	
Ramsay's (North Carolina) Battery	
Cabell's Battalion	Col. Henry C. Cabell
Callaway's (Georgia) Battery	
Carlton's (Georgia) Battery	
McCarthy's (Virginia) Battery	
Manly's (North Carolina) Battery	

II CORPS	LT. GEN. RICHARD S. EWELL
Early's Division	Maj. Gen. Jubal A. Early
Hays' Brigade	Brig. Gen. Harry T. Hays
5th Louisiana	Lt. Col. Bruce Menger
6th Louisiana	Maj. William H. Manning
7th Louisiana	Maj. J. Moore Wilson
8th Louisiana	
9th Louisiana	
Pegram's Brigade	Brig. Gen. John Pegram
13th Virginia	Col. James B. Terrill
31st Virginia	Col. John S. Hoffman
49th Virginia	Col. J. Catlett Gibson
52nd Virginia	
58th Virginia	
Gordon's Brigade	Brig. Gen. John B. Gordon
13th Georgia	
26th Georgia	Col. Edmund N. Atkinson
31st Georgia	Col. Clement A. Evans
38th Georgia	
60th Georgia	Lt. Col. Thomas J. Berry
61st Georgia	

Johnson's Division	**Maj. Gen. Edward Johnson**
Stonewall Brigade	Brig. Gen. James A. Walker
2nd Virginia	Capt. Charles H. Stewart
4th Virginia	Col. William Terry
5th Virginia	
27th Virginia	Lt. Col. Charles L. Haynes
33rd Virginia	
Jones' Brigade	Brig. Gen. John M. Jones
21st Virginia	
25th Virginia	Col. John C. Higginbotham
42nd Virginia	
44th Virginia	
48th Virginia	
50th Virginia	
Steuart's Brigade	Brig. Gen. George H. Steuart
1st North Carolina	Col. Hamilton A. Brown
3rd North Carolina	Col. Stephen D. Thruston
10th Virginia	
23rd Virginia	
37th Virginia	
Stafford's Brigade	Brig. Gen. Leroy A. Stafford
1st Louisiana	
2nd Louisiana	Col. Jesse M. Williams
10th Louisiana	
14th Louisiana	
15th Louisiana	
Rodes' Division	**Maj. Gen. Robert E. Rodes**
Daniel's Brigade	Brig. Gen. Junius Daniel
32nd North Carolina	
43rd North Carolina	
45th North Carolina	
53rd North Carolina	
2nd North Carolina Battalion	
Doles' Brigade	Brig. Gen. George Doles
4th Georgia	
12th Georgia	Col. Edward Willis
44th Georgia	Col. William H. Peebles
Ramseur's Brigade	Brig. Gen. Stephen D. Ramseur
2nd North Carolina	Col. William R. Cox
4th North Carolina	Col. Bryan Grimes
14th North Carolina	Col. R. Tyler Bennett
30th North Carolina	Col. Francis M. Parker
Battle's Brigade	Brig. Gen. Cullen A. Battle
3rd Alabama	Col. Charles Forsyth
5th Alabama	
6th Alabama	
12th Alabama	
26th Alabama	
Johnston's Brigade	Brig. Gen. Robert D. Johnston
5th North Carolina	Col. Thomas M. Garrett
12th North Carolina	Col. Henry E. Coleman

20th North Carolina	Col. Thomas F. Toon
23rd North Carolina	
Artillery	**Brig. Gen. Armistead L. Long**
Hardaway's Battalion	Lt. Col. Robert A. Hardaway
Dance's (Virginia) Battery	
Graham's (Virginia) Battery	
Griffin's C. B. (Virginia) Battery	
Jones' (Virginia) Battery	
Smith's B. H. (Virginia) Battery	
Braxton's Battalion	Lt. Col. Carter M. Braxton
Carpenter's (Virginia) Battery	
Cooper's (Virginia) Battery	
Hardwicke's (Virginia) Battery	
Nelson's Battalion	Lt. Col. William Nelson
Kirkpatrick's (Virginia) Battery	
Massie's (Virginia) Battery	
Milledge's (Georgia) Battery	
Cutshaw's Battalion	Maj. Wilfred E. Cutshaw
Carrington's (Virginia) Battery	
Garber's A. W. (Virginia) Battery	
Tanner's (Virginia) Battery	
Page's Battalion	Maj. Richard C. M. Page
Carter's W. P. (Virginia) Battery	
Fry's (Virginia) Battery	
Page's (Virginia) Battery	
Reese's (Alabama) Battery	

III CORPS	**LT. GEN. AMBROSE P. HILL (REPLACED BY JUBAL EARLY AFTER THE WILDERNESS DUE TO ILLNESS)**
Anderson's Division	**Maj. Gen. Richard H. Anderson**
Perrin's Brigade	Brig. Gen. Abner Perrin
8th Alabama	
9th Alabama	
10th Alabama	
11th Alabama	
14th Alabama	
Harris' Brigade	Brig. Gen. Nathaniel H. Harris
12th Mississippi	
16th Mississippi	Col. Samuel E. Baker
19th Mississippi	Col. Thomas J. Hardin
48th Mississippi	
Mahone's Brigade	Brig. Gen. William Mahone
6th Virginia	Lt. Col. Henry W. Williamson
12th Virginia	Col. David A. Weisiger
16th Virginia	Lt. Col. Richard O. Whitehead
41st Virginia	
61st Virginia	Col. Virginius D. Groner
Wright's Brigade	Brig. Gen. Ambrose R. Wright
3rd Georgia	
22nd Georgia	

48th Georgia
2nd Georgia Battalion — Maj. Charles J. Moffett
Perry's Brigade — Brig. Gen. Edward A. Perry
  2nd Florida
  5th Florida
  8th Florida

Heth's Division — **Maj. Gen. Henry Heth**
Davis' Brigade — Brig. Gen. Joseph R. Davis
  2nd Mississippi
  11th Mississippi
  42nd Mississippi
  55th North Carolina
Cooke's Brigade — Brig. Gen. John R. Cooke
  15th North Carolina
  27th North Carolina
  46th North Carolina
  48th North Carolina
Kirkland's Brigade — Brig. Gen. William W. Kirkland
  11th North Carolina
  26th North Carolina
  44th North Carolina
  47th North Carolina
  52nd North Carolina
Walker's Brigade — Brig. Gen. Henry H. Walker
  40th Virginia
  47th Virginia — Col. Robert M. Mayo
  55th Virginia — Col. William S. Christian
  22nd Virginia Battalion
Archer's Brigade — Brig. Gen. James J. Archer
  13th Alabama
  1st Tennessee (Provisional Army) — Maj. Felix G. Buchanan
  7th Tennessee — Lt. Col. Samuel G. Shepard
  14th Tennessee — Col. William McComb

Wilcox's Division — **Maj. Gen. Cadmus M. Wilcox**
Lane's Brigade — Brig. Gen. James H. Lane
  7th North Carolina — Lt. Col. William Lee Davidson
  18th North Carolina — Col. John D. Barry
  28th North Carolina
  33rd North Carolina — Lt. Col. Robert V. Cowan
  37th North Carolina — Col. William M. Barbour
Scales' Brigade — Brig. Gen. Alfred M. Scales
  13th North Carolina — Col. Joseph H. Hyman
  16th North Carolina — Col. William A. Stowe
  22nd North Carolina
  34th North Carolina — Col. William L. J. Lowrance
  38th North Carolina — Lt. Col. John Ashford
McGowan's Brigade — Brig. Gen. Samuel McGowan
  1st South Carolina (Provisional Army) — Lt. Col. Washington P. Shooter
  12th South Carolina — Col. John L. Miller
  13th South Carolina — Col. Benjamin T. Brockman

14th South Carolina — Col. Joseph N. Brown
1st South Carolina (Orr's Rifles) — Lt. Col. George Mcd. Miller
Thomas' Brigade — Brig. Gen. Edward R. Thomas
  14th Georgia
  35th Georgia
  45th Georgia
  49th Georgia — Lt. Col. John T. Jordan
Artillery — **Col. R. Lindsay Walker**
Poague's Battalion — Lt. Col. William T. Poague
  Richards' (Mississippi) Battery
  Utterback's (Virginia) Battery
  Williams' (North Carolina) Battery
  Wyatt's (Virginia) Battery
Pegram's Battalion — Lt. Col. William J. Pegram
  Brander's (Virginia) Battery
  Cayce's (Virginia) Battery
  Ellett's (Virginia) Battery
  Marye's (Virginia) Battery
  Zimmerman's (South Carolina) Battery
McIntosh's Battalion — Lt. Col. David G. McIntosh
  Clutter's (Virginia) Battery
  Donald's (Virginia) Battery
  Hurt's (Alabama) Battery
  Price's (Virginia) Battery
Cutts' Battalion — Col. Allen S. Cutts
  Patterson's (Georgia) Battery
  Ross' (Georgia) Battery
  Wingfield's (Georgia) Battery
Richardson's Battalion — Lt. Col. Charles Richardson
  Grandy's (Virginia) Battery
  Landry's (Louisiana) Battery
  Moore's (Virginia) Battery
  Penick's (Virginia) Battery

CAVALRY CORPS — **MAJ. GEN. JAMES E. B. STUART**
Hampton's Division — **Maj. Gen. Wade Hampton**
Young's Brigade — Brig. Gen. Pierce M. B. Young
  7th Georgia — Col. William P. White
  Cobb's (Georgia) Legion — Col. G. J. Wright
  Phillips' (Georgia) Legion
  20th Georgia Battalion — Lt. Col. John M. Millen
  Jeff. Davis (Mississippi) Legion
Rosser's Brigade — Brig. Gen. Thomas L. Rosser
  7th Virginia — Col. Richard H. Dulany
  11th Virginia
  12th Virginia — Lt. Col. Thomas B. Massie
  35th Virginia Battalion
Butler's Brigade — Brig. Gen. Matthew C. Butler
  4th South Carolina — Col. B. Huger Rutledge
  5th South Carolina — Col. John Dunovant
  6th South Carolina — Col. Hugh K. Aiken

THE BATTLES OF THE WILDERNESS AND SPOTSYLVANIA

GRANT CROSSES THE RAPIDAN

As midnight approached on May 3 various commanders rousted their subordinates who woke up the rest of the chain of command and the pre-planned march route to the fords began. Brigadier-General David Gregg's cavalry was up ahead, securing the fords and protecting the engineers who labored to construct pontoon bridges and prepared roads for the massive numbers of men and wagons to follow.

Winfield Scott Hancock's corps was to cross at Ely's Ford and was within a couple of miles of its objective when day broke. John Sedgwick's and Gouvernor Warren's corps crossed at Germanna Ford, Sedgwick not leaving until 4am on the 4th in order to fall in behind Warren. Brigadier-General James Wilson's cavalry got into a brief skirmish with some Rebel cavalry at the Germanna Ford, but otherwise there was no serious opposition to the advance to the fords.

Both wings of the main army began crossing the pontoon bridges by 6am on May 4, a massive sea of blue streaming toward Lee. Meade himself crossed around 9.30am with Grant making it over by noon. The two camped near each other at a local farmhouse. Though tiring under their loads, the Union troops headed out in a smooth fashion. Hancock was satisfied and made camp just beyond Chancellorsville a bit before 10am, while the tail of

This photo shows the Army of the Potomac artillery crossing the Rapidan at Germanna Ford. The Wilderness provided few openings for massed artillery barrages. (Library of Congress)

John Sedgwick was a veteran leader, unafraid to take aggressive action and personally taking to the front in order to boost morale. (Library of Congress)

Union soldiers passing through the battlefields of Chancellorsville toward the Wilderness came upon grim reminders of last year's deadly struggle. (Library of Congress)

his II Corps was across by early afternoon. Warren and Sedgwick found no opposition and set up near Wilderness Tavern. Grant believed the first phase of his plan to have been successful at 2pm when the last unit was over the Rapidan.

An examination of what Lee was doing is in order. He showed little activity to Union scouts until 11am when he got some coded signal flag messages that indicated a Union shift toward the old Mine Run position. If Lee was worried about the odds, he didn't show it and the Union vanguard was skirmishing on the Orange Turnpike as early as 1pm. Once Warren was firmly ensconced at Wilderness Tavern, Wilson's troopers moved out to the next objective, a place called Parker's Store, finding little sign of Rebels.

However, by 3pm, reports came that Lee was finally moving from his battlements. Wilson, buoyed by the lack of resistance, believed he had enough patrols out to cover the approaches to the Union position. He was wrong.

He had left Orange Turnpike unattended. Warren's V Corps was there, what amounted to the right end of the Union line. On the right end of this corps was Charles Griffin's 1st Division. His men, exhausted by their march, just wanted to get some sleep. Pickets were thrown out haphazardly. Reports of distant campfires were disregarded as those of Wilson's cavalry. Sedgwick came up behind Warren and the two corps were acting as if the enemy were far, far away. Hancock was at Chancellorsville, discovering grisly remains and debris from last year's battle where "Fighting Joe" Hooker was brought low by Lee.

Supply wagons began to trundle across newly constructed wooden bridges after 5pm and the Union Army seemed content. Grant was especially pleased that the first day's objectives had been reached without serious loss of life. For his men, surrounded by the dark, deep curtains of dense growth, it was

a different story. Staring at the empty eye sockets of skulls that they dug up while making preparations, the Union troops were uneasy, falling asleep with the belief that Lee was out there, waiting.

Lee, however, waited for no enemy. He had a good idea of Grant's possibilities as early as May 2. Scouts and deserters helped the flow of information also. Very early on May 4, the direction of advance became clear, just not its objective. Cavalry could see the long blue rivulets of men followed by their wagons, but would they head south or swing to hit Fredericksburg from behind? Lee mulled things over and decided his Rapidan line was compromised. It was time to see what he could do to the Yankees.

Once he was sure that there was no second pincer toward the Liberty Mills area, he called on Ewell to get ready to come forward around 1am. As dawn arrived, so did confirmation of Grant's approach and axis of advance. It was time to put the army into motion. Seeing the situation, Lee decided to assemble his army along his old Mine Run line and sent orders to Hill and Longstreet. Both were to advance along the same road and Longstreet worried about congestion, so Lee allowed him to shift his route, but it would still leave him hours behind Hill. Without Longstreet's corps, Lee would be outnumbered three to one if Grant threw in his entire army plus IX Corps.

Ambrose Hill was a dogged opponent, famous for his red shirt. He was used to hard campaigning, but illness was slowing him down. (University of Kentucky)

Longstreet sent assurances that he would be in the line by noon on May 5, no matter the distance. He got hold of a guide on the evening of May 4 but his men were struggling to get to the camp that evening, which was some

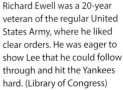

Richard Ewell was a 20-year veteran of the regular United States Army, where he liked clear orders. He was eager to show Lee that he could follow through and hit the Yankees hard. (Library of Congress)

16 miles from the planned Brock's Bridge bivouac area. Longstreet's timetable was in need of some adjustment. Lee, camped near Rhodes House, waited to see what Grant's next move would be. Finding no firm answer from scouts, Lee decided to provoke Grant to see what sort of response he would get.

He picked Ewell to advance in the hope of catching the Federals strung out and tied up in the Wilderness, with the idea of causing them a lot of trouble. If that failed, he could fall back to Mine Run. After all, Longstreet would be up by noon, he was told. If Ewell could crush the Union flank, Longstreet could then roll up the whole army and another promising Union general could be sent back across the Potomac in disgrace.

Disquieting news from Richmond drew off some of Lee's enthusiasm. Union Major-General Ben Butler was disembarking over 30,000 men on the James River and Major-General Franz Sigel was moving out of Winchester, Virginia, heading down the Shenandoah Valley. Lee sent a cable to Major-General John C. Breckinridge, an ex-Vice President of the United States, to stop Sigel, but Richmond clawed back two brigades coming to Lee in order to stymie Butler. Lee tried to get them back by pointing out that Major-General P. G. T. Beauregard had troops to spare in North Carolina to help

defend Richmond against Butler. President Davis could not be moved, though, and Beauregard pled illness. This in no way dissuaded Lee.

Scouts arrived before dawn to let Lee know that Grant was coming straight across Lee's front through the Wilderness. Lee was unfazed by the prospect of over 100,000 men slamming into his position and it's possible he had no clue Grant had that many men. He had little idea of Grant's stubbornness and felt that his opponent had thrown away the advantage of numbers by choosing to march through the Wilderness. Lee was determined to teach him a lesson, given some luck and Longstreet. For this day, he had to hold, and with the arrival of Longstreet, strike back on the 6th.

Grant, camped not far away from the coming battle, was pleased with what news came to him. Major-General Sherman's advance east had begun in earnest, Butler had landed at Bermuda Hundred on the James and was marching, while Sigel was also moving. He sat down with Meade to get his piece of the puzzle going. Meade was already nervous about the army being spread out and exposed. He had heard reports that Confederate cavalry was not far from Fredericksburg and subordinated a huge amount of cavalry to protect his precious wagons as they plodded along the supply lines. This would have consequences, reducing the cavalry screens that protected Union flanks and scouted for Lee's main thrust. The Union Army was going into battle half-blind.

Instead of moving toward Mine Run as Lee hoped, Grant and Meade settled on a semicircular formation through the Wilderness, resuming pressure on Lee when Burnside's corps was in position. This meant that the Union advance would come to a planned halt, destroying any sense of initiative and revealing Meade's typical hesitancy to commit troops to a robust offensive until all his units were assembled. Memory of the Mine Run battle remained strong and Meade assumed Lee would fight there again. This time, Meade would have Lee outflanked by going through the Wilderness, outnumbered, outgunned and out-horsed. Grant was expecting a fight on the 5th and he was right, but it wasn't the fight either side envisioned.

The Union Army had squandered all its advantages by moving into the tangled mess of the Wilderness. Numerical superiority was meaningless if the enemy could not be found. Cannon were confined to firing along the narrow roads and worse, Meade had drained off his cavalry superiority, guarding against a threat that never materialized.

MAY 5 – DAY ONE OF THE BATTLE

The order of the day from Grant was simple. Two roads ran parallel toward Lee, the Orange Turnpike and the Orange Plank Road. Meade's force was to spread out into a line between them and hit Lee wherever he was found. Hancock was on the left end of the Union line and Warren on the right, with Sedgwick to come up behind Warren and move to the right of his line, Charles Griffin's division, while Burnside would fill in where needed. James Wadsworth was to support Griffin's left flank with his division.

Hancock was delayed by Meade's redeployment of the Union cavalry, so Warren's corps started toward Todd's Tavern but the hot day and entangling brush sapped the strength from his men until many passed out from exertion. Wadsworth was finding the land between the roads to be marshy, and where

The first day of the Wilderness, May 5, around noon

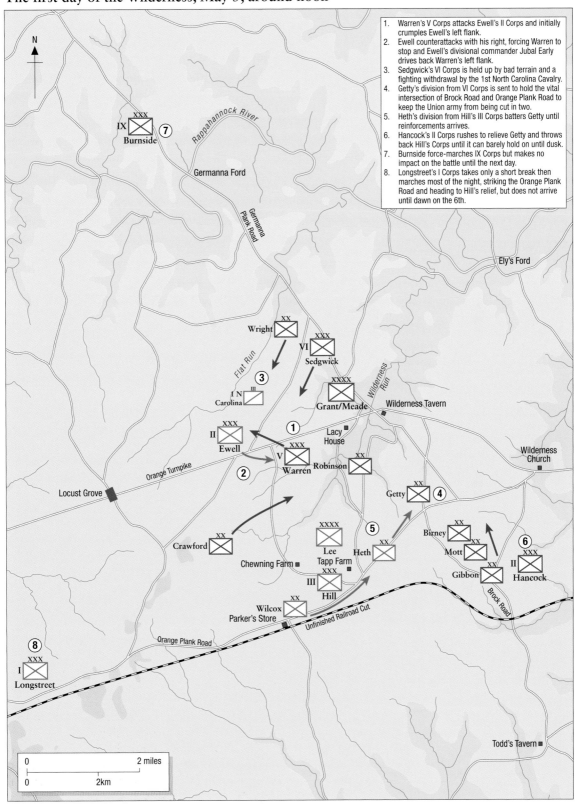

1. Warren's V Corps attacks Ewell's II Corps and initially crumples Ewell's left flank.
2. Ewell counterattacks with his right, forcing Warren to stop and Ewell's divisional commander Jubal Early drives back Warren's left flank.
3. Sedgwick's VI Corps is held up by bad terrain and a fighting withdrawal by the 1st North Carolina Cavalry.
4. Getty's division from VI Corps is sent to hold the vital intersection of Brock Road and Orange Plank Road to keep the Union army from being cut in two.
5. Heth's division from Hill's III Corps batters Getty until reinforcements arrives.
6. Hancock's II Corps rushes to relieve Getty and throws back Hill's Corps until it can barely hold on until dusk.
7. Burnside force-marches IX Corps but makes no impact on the battle until the next day.
8. Longstreet's I Corps takes only a short break then marches most of the night, striking the Orange Plank Road and heading to Hill's relief, but does not arrive until dawn on the 6th.

it was not marshy it was so dense his men had to hack trails using whatever axes and hatchets they could scrounge. Infantry pickets fanned out to find the Rebels, but it was all a green, oppressive hell.

Suddenly, there was a report of Rebels in the woods near Orange Turnpike. Warren ignored this at first, thinking it some dismounted cavalry sent to delay him, but another report came in from Griffin, who Warren knew was a levelheaded general who didn't exaggerate. Warren needed time to sort things out and ordered Griffin to hold the road until Sedgwick could come alongside and try to get a handle on how large a force was ahead. This was carried out by Colonel Joseph Hayes, who pushed out a line of skirmishers from the two regiments he commanded. Coming to the edge of a clearing called Saunders' Field, he stopped and saw men in butternut digging a trench line on the other side of the field.

Meade, hearing the news, ordered Warren to stop and deal with the Rebels, then ordered Hancock to halt also. Even though Meade assumed the Confederates were a delaying force, his caution allowed his entire grand advance to stop, inviting the very situation he and Grant planned to avoid – a battle in the Wilderness with the various corps strung out. Grant told Meade not to wait to get sorted out and to "pitch into" the Confederates right away, which suited Meade, as long as he could get Warren's flanks straight. It should have happened with Sedgwick's VI Corps on the right and Wadsworth watching Griffin's left, but the ground would not support rapid movement. Meade was trying to get his line straight and do the job right, especially since Grant was present.

Confederate cavalry were armed with single shot carbines for long-range battles, while the Union cavalry carried the Spencer repeating carbine, an important force multiplier on the defensive. Here are two troopers holding their Spencers. (Library of Congress)

Any forward progress was finished by 8am. Warren could not get his line suited, which was fine by Lee. He was jamming his two available corps down the same roads as the Yankees heading toward him, turning a delaying action into a corps-sized defensive position with another corps (Hill's) poised to hit Warren's flank as soon as it could be found. Meanwhile, Meade was furious at the lack of warning from Wilson, whose cavalry were otherwise occupied.

Lee was shifting troops around and hitting Meade where it wasn't expected. If the Union Army didn't form a cohesive line soon, it would be another Chancellorsville. Meade was blind, his army strung out for miles and Lee had massed two corps in the worst possible place, far from the sort of set-piece battle that Meade preferred. Wilson and his cavalry misread Meade's intent and assumed, with infantry arriving, his men could move on. So at the critical spot for a flank move, only the 5th New York Cavalry under Lt. Col. John Hammond was watching the Orange Plank Road. While the rest headed down Catharpin Road, Hammond got about 2 miles from Parker's Store and was confronted first by some cavalry and then the lead elements of Henry Heth's division.

Hammond deployed his men, but their repeating rifles could not entirely make up for the lack of numbers, though they did make one of Hill's aides believe a whole brigade was engaging them. Warren's 3rd Division under Crawford was forming up nearby on Chewning Heights, imploring Hammond to hold on, but it was too much to expect a regiment to stop a corps.

Tearing loose, Hammond's troopers retreated from the Parker's Store area and back up to Brock Road. If Hill could get the Brock Road clear, he and Ewell would crush Warren. Brigadier-General George Getty with Sedgwick's 2nd Division arrived just in time to hold the road. There was still the matter of Hancock's II Corps coming up. He needed a clear road and very nearly didn't get it.

James Wilson, Hammond's 3rd Cavalry Division commander, was heading west on Catharpin Road when he ran smack into Rosser's Cavalry Brigade, part of Wade Hampton's division, near Craig's Meeting House. He charged in, but Rosser's men were veterans and it took a tough series of actions to force Rosser back beyond the Faulkner House where Wilson set up shop, placing his horse artillery at Craig's Meeting House. His respite was short lived as Rosser flanked one of his brigades, sending it back in confusion. This brigade, Chapman's, fled behind the next one, Bryan's. Backed by Federal field artillery, they stood firm for a moment, but the battle broke and swirled all around their position, forcing Wilson to disengage and flee eastward along Catharpin Road.

Meanwhile, David Gregg's 2nd Cavalry Division was deploying to meet Wilson along the Catharpin Road at Todd's Tavern. He met Rosser head on, slamming the gray troopers back. His victory didn't last, as a brigade from Fitzhugh Lee's Cavalry Division showed up on the Brock Road and suddenly the Union cavalry on Grant's left was out of action, hemmed in on two sides by Confederates. They had played little part in the day's actions other than to get into a pointless battle that left them unable to help the Union cause.

Things were no better with the Union II and V Corps pushing through the Wilderness. Crawford, who sat on an excellent piece of high ground, nevertheless abandoned it to return to the line of battle that Warren had earlier indicated. This widened the gap between Hancock and the rest of the army. It was a hole similar to that which Longstreet saw open up months earlier at Chickamauga. Could Lee take advantage of it?

The Confederate commander pondered the matter over breakfast that day. Lee dearly hoped to keep Grant's army busy with a deadly game of blind-man's-bluff until Longstreet arrived. He was ready to take Grant's measure, believing a second Chancellorsville was possible. If he could avoid uneven odds by keeping Hancock busy with Stuart's cavalry, so much the better. If not, the war could be lost that afternoon.

Ewell stopped at the edge of Saunders' Field. He deployed Edward Johnson's division on high ground with Robert Rodes' division just behind him and Jubal Early's in reserve. Fifteen thousand Confederates prepared to deploy as soon as Warren's corps appeared in strength. Hill was also moving along, with Heth's division in sight of the Brock Road a bit after 8am.

Here is Waud's depiction of Grant and Meade conferring at Lacy House, Warren's headquarters at the Wilderness. Waud has written July 5 for some reason and made notes for the engravers who would turn his sketch into artwork for newspapers. The battle rages in the distance. (Library of Congress)

Brigadier-General Horatio Wright would eventually replace Sedgwick. Wright was a competent leader, but he had a tough task to fill the void left by his predecessor. (Library of Congress)

By noon, he was engaging Getty's division. Believing the Union would advance no further, Lee moved his headquarters behind Hill's corps to the Widow Tapp's Farm, along with a number of artillery batteries. All he had to do was wait for Longstreet and then he could roll up Grant. He had no idea that four Union divisions were deployed in the woods in front of him. Lee was nearly undone when a line of blue-jacketed infantry stumbled out of those woods, but seeing the Confederates, the Yankees withdrew, not realizing that they could have decapitated most of the Rebel command structure with a few volleys.

Ewell was still sorting out his deployment to prepare for Meade as the latter was trying to untangle enough of his army to start the attack. Growing tired of waiting for Burnside's IX Corps, Grant rode forward to find Meade at Lacy House around 10am. From this position they tried to get a handle on the battle as Grant tweaked Meade's dispositions. He became concerned that Meade was turning his advance into a static defensive position and his orders showed an obsession with his flanks. When Warren came up to meet with them, he did nothing to dispel Meade's uncertainty. Confederates seemed to be behind every tree the V Corps commander examined. Grant was appalled at the sight of so many experienced generals dissolving into confusion.

He could resist the urge to intervene no longer. Certain that his massive numbers would prevail he directed a series of orders through Meade with machine-gun-like rapidity. Hancock was too far away to do anything about Hill, so he took Getty from Sedgwick to hold the vital Brock Road intersection as explained above. Warren and the rest of Sedgwick's men were to attack from whatever locations their divisions were in without waiting to form a cohesive line. Daylight was slipping toward noon and it was time to fight.

At the other end of the battle, Hammond's dogged retreat over a mile allowed Getty to cover the 2 miles to the intersection in the nick of time, barely getting in position to keep Heth away. Grant ordered Hancock's advance redirected toward the Brock Road intersection, straight at Hill. The II Corps commander had 4 miles to

A Waud depiction of VI Corps on the first day. He notes some rifle pits to the right and a battery of Massachusetts artillery on the left. (Library of Congress)

cover while Getty's division had to hold off an entire corps. He was doing it, though, and so that flank was settled for the time being. Grant next looked to his right flank.

Wright's 1st Division from Sedgwick's corps marched down the Spottswood Road (on some maps it is the Spotswood Road, Flat Run Road or Culpepper Mine Road), covering Warren's right flank. Warren's men slowly moved out, sad to leave their prepared positions and, tender about their exposed flanks, regardless of Meade's orders, tried to form a line anyway, hampered by the dense woods. By noon, there was little to show for their efforts aside from sniping and skirmishing. Warren churned out order after order to his brigade commanders, but they were unwilling to march into the rows of trees and curtains of brush where unknown numbers of veteran Rebels awaited them. Ricketts came up to watch Wright's flank, and Warren finally got enough men forward to start a real battle around 1pm. Griffin slashed forward in two lines with Wadsworth to his left. Ayres' and Bartlett's brigades moved halfway across Saunders' Field as Steuart's and Jones' brigades chewed them up. Men went down in heaps along a small gully and the first attack line was finished. Two more Rebel brigades waited on Steuart's left, firing obliquely into the blue masses. The second line went forward, including the 146th New York Zouaves, resplendent targets in red trousers for Ewell's men to aim at.

Men dropped everywhere and "Maryland" Steuart's (so named to differentiate him from Jeb Stuart) units rose from their trenches to hurl back the 140th New York at the point of their bayonets as they went in with the Zouaves. The din of battle, heavy smoke and thick underbrush turned the Union advance into a cauldron of chaos. Worse, the Rebels were starting to flank Griffin's right. Bartlett fared no better until reinforced, then he struck Brigadier-General John Jones' Virginia Brigade hard. Both Jones and his aide were killed and his men started to retreat. Things were looking up for the Union advance and Bartlett kept moving up until his men were a surging, disorganized mass.

Bartlett could not know that he was advancing alone. Ayres had been stopped cold. Confederate muskets thundered along their right flank, their intensity growing as Jones' men re-formed. Soon, the blue tide was ebbing back to their starting positions with Ewell's men in full pursuit. Bartlett barely escaped with his life. Once Griffin's attack was finished Ewell then turned to Wadsworth.

The 4th Division of Warren's corps contained the famous Iron Brigade under Cutler, and they moved alongside of Mill Branch. The branch isolated him from the rest of Wadsworth's men and he was soon taking heavy fire from his right. Ewell, mindful of Lee's orders not to get sucked into a heavy engagement, became concerned for his own flanks and requested John B. Gordon's brigade of Georgians to reinforce the front, and Jubal Early dutifully sent for him. The grim general spurred his horse forward, sword in hand, his brigade close behind.

They slammed full force into Cutler's brigade, already worn down through fighting with Confederates under Battle and Dole. Deafened by the crash of guns and hit by howling Georgians, the unsupported Cutler and his veterans bent inward, allowing Gordon to cut them in half and roll them up. To avoid destruction they plunged back on top of Denison's Maryland Brigade. The butternut thunderbolt rocked them back also, leaving Wadsworth's right flank desperately clinging to the Lacy House area as they tried to re-form.

Roy Stone's brigade was bogged down in swampy ground below Spring Hill. Struggling in muddy water, they got misaligned badly and became easy targets. After a while, they, too, fled to safety, leaving only Rice's brigade. His unit was badly positioned also and was hit by Junius Daniel's brigade as it seemingly appeared by magic from the thick underbrush. The Rebels' initial volley was decimating and Rice's men buckled like Cutler's and Stone's.

Daniels chased them all the way to Lacy House before being stopped. William McCandless's brigade was thrown in to settle things down for Warren but it was to no avail. Instead, he advanced into enfilade and lost the entire 7th Pennsylvania Regiment as prisoners in a ruse by the 61st Georgia Regiment, who convinced them an entire brigade was opposing them.

The rest of the afternoon was spent jockeying for position. Both sides formed trench lines and fired continuous volleys from them. The flame from hundreds of muzzles ignited the tinder lying on the woods' floor, sending a wall of flame from Ewell's earthworks across Saunders' Field. The conflagration killed the wounded and turned corpses to heaps of blackened flesh.

Warren's attack was in a shambles. Meade had pushed him forward in haste and the awful terrain of the Wilderness scattered his men so that no cohesive line could be formed. Ewell, to his credit, had played a careful, yet aggressive hand, defeated the Union formations in detail, capturing hundreds of men and several pieces of artillery.

Grant remained relatively calm on hearing the results, trying not to let his frustration show, but it

The sheer volume of rifle fire blasting through the Wilderness set off numerous fires and soldiers risked their lives to carry their wounded comrades to safety. Not all were successful. (Library of Congress)

nearly boiled over when Griffin rode up and berated Wright and Warren. It took Meade's personal intervention to keep the man from arrest. Sucked into a fight where he did not want it, Grant's instinct was to keep Ewell and Hill engaged while superior numbers could be brought to bear. Hancock was not up yet to fall upon Hill, and Burnside's command was still marching, likely to end up exhausted upon arrival. Grant went up for a look and found Sedgwick's corps getting into position, but that position wasn't the best.

Led by Horatio Wright, Sedgwick's 1st Division had four brigades formed up astride the Spottswood Road, connecting with Warren's units at Orange Turnpike. A combination of the terrain and Confederate delaying tactics were hindering his deployment, including some fires deliberately set to block him. Waiting for him were three Rebel brigades, one of them the veteran Stonewall Brigade.

By 3pm they were engaged and it was more of the same as Warren's brigades had faced, except this time it was the Stonewall Brigade that ended up being isolated. Leroy Stafford's Louisiana troops tried to reconnect but became confused and were forced into a ragged retreat back to their trenches with Stafford suffering a paralyzing bullet wound. A reserve brigade under Harry Hays from Jubal Early's division filled the gap, only to be thrown back with heavy loss. It took the personal appearance of Early himself to keep the line together.

The Confederates held, but barely, frantically carving out new earthworks. Unable to make headway, Wright's men did the same. By 5pm the battle to dislodge Ewell had failed. Grant, in his eagerness to overwhelm Ewell, had sent his units forward in a fragmented fashion, inviting defeat in detail.

Undaunted, Grant tried to make his plan work. He left orders for Burnside to hurry along, even though IX Corps had been in motion since 6pm the day before, their advance staggered to protect the supply lines from raids by Confederate guerrilla cavalry under Colonel John Singleton Mosby. Had they been sent forward immediately instead of spaced out, those 20,000 men would have made a difference. Burnside received the order and responded enthusiastically, driving his men forward until they were able to make it to the front by 2pm. There they sat while Wright smashed against the Confederate line without help.

What happened? We may never know for sure, but Grant wanted Burnside to support Wright. He sent him a message to that effect at 3pm. For some reason, communications broke down and the decisive weight of Burnside was never used. The chain of command was too vague for the coordination Grant desired.

This Currier and Ives print gives the idea that the battle was fought in the open in ranks, which it was not; it was a savage battle in dense undergrowth. (Library of Congress)

Grant was having no better luck south along the Orange Plank Road. Meade was trying to stop Hancock at Todd's Tavern and reroute him to the Orange Plank Road–Brock Road intersection, but the note was not received until 9am and Hancock was 2 miles beyond that landmark. Uncertain, Hancock stopped II Corps in place and waited for more orders. It took another two hours for confirmation that he was to move to the intersection of Orange Plank and Brock Roads. This was bad news since Hancock was lined up along the Catharpin Road, going west. His entire corps had to be turned, sorted out, and sent 4 miles up the Brock Road.

Hancock reached the beleaguered Getty at noon and then asked for new orders. Meade sent word to attack immediately and link up with Warren, sending the orders at 1.30pm though they took until 2.30pm to reach Hancock. By then Hancock had two divisions at hand, but Meade was under the impression it was the entire II Corps. Things went downhill from there.

At 3.45pm, Meade sent clear orders for Getty to attack immediately and for Hancock to support him with two divisions. A little before 4pm Getty had his brigades formed into attack columns and attacked westward along the Orange Plank Road, leaving Hancock's men to try to get in position and support him after the fact.

The overgrown, washboard terrain, shot through with swampy bottomland, was awful on the advance, but well suited to Henry Heth's dug in Rebels. Hill's other division under Cadmus Wilcox was behind Heth and trying to bridge the gap between Hill's and Ewell's corps by sliding north. Heth, uncertain whether to advance to drive off the unknown Yankees in front of him, was soon assaulted by Getty, whose men fell quickly to the gray sharpshooters at ranges up to 300 yards.

The advance was stopped cold. Hancock's men rushed to the sounds of battle as Getty implored him for support. Major-General David Birney's 3rd Division of II Corps arrived first with Brigadier-General Gershom Mott's 4th Division coming along behind. Birney's brigades went forward from the Brock Road, to be stopped as well by Heth's line sliding over to unload on them. Mott came into position after 4pm and his men spent half an hour constructing hasty breastworks before getting the order to advance. Heth was now outnumbered three to one but far from outmaneuvered.

Mott's two brigades jammed themselves between the trees, being herded into an ever-thicker mass as the paths of advance narrowed. As such, they were impossible to miss. Flame rippled across their front in two massive volleys, dropping men amid a flurry of clipped leaves. The fight left Mott's division altogether. Unable to recover after the first volley, the units fell back and ran for their breastworks.

Here is the intersection of the Orange Plank and Brock Roads as it looks today. Even now, only a few yards from the roadside, thick forest abounds. Its shadows hid enemies and made friends look like foes. (Author's photograph)

Reserves moved up to stop the pursuing Confederates and sent them reeling back. Things settled down a bit, but Getty continued trying to keep up the pressure on Heth and could make no headway. Birney, undaunted, tossed in Alexander Hays' brigade. Hays ran into flashes of musketry and a wall of smoke before falling with a bullet in his brain.

Aides streamed from the front to Hancock, struggling amid the filthy, bloody refugees. More troops, they begged. Hancock waited for Gibbon's 2nd Division to come up. Meanwhile, the II Corps leader rode back and forth to stem the retreating mob of bluecoats from Mott's division. Two of Gibbon's brigades arrived and Hancock shoved them toward Birney. Just in time, as the victorious Rebels were advancing again to try to seize the Brock Road. Gibbon, along with his remaining brigade, appeared and they hurled themselves into the woods near the intersection to stop the Confederate breakthrough.

Heth could push no further. The weight of Union numbers, regardless of the terrain, were shoving him inexorably backward, leaving a wake of dead and dying. Hancock was starting to get a handle on his front. His skilled mind knew he had the numbers and while the Rebels could send volley after volley to break up his advance, they couldn't be everywhere. He was patiently waiting for Barlow, his last division commander, when a problem arose.

A captured enemy prisoner had talked tough about how Longstreet was coming up to smash into the Union left. Intelligence agreed; Longstreet was supposed to be doing just that. Hancock was going to use Barlow to flank Heth, but if I Corps charged up the Catharpin Road and swept away the small covering force Hancock maintained at Todd's Tavern, Hancock could be in big trouble.

The Confederate I Corps commander was far behind his own ambitious schedule and it would be hours before his weight could be felt. In the interim, the remaining two corps would be in major trouble if Meade realized. Heth would soon be fending off 30,000 men. He was out of reserves and Hancock seemed to have an endless stream of brigades to throw at him. Lee had to come up with something or Hill's corps was doomed.

He recalled Wilcox's under-strength division from its march to link with Ewell. Lee hoped the Yankees wouldn't notice the gap. The brigades of Alfred Scales and Samuel McGowan were resting nearby so he ordered them across Widow Tapp's Farm to fill in the thinning gray line. Heth was fending off four divisions with a fifth on its way. However, in character with Southern tactics, Wilcox and Heth wanted to attack with these two brigades, but the units became separated and were forced back. There were simply not enough men to drive off the Union soldiers. Hill's entire corps was in serious jeopardy by 6pm.

The huge casualties and fear of Longstreet, though, were starting to worry Hancock. Grant wanted action and seized on the reversal of Wilcox's division to reinforce Heth. He mistook this countermarch as Lee taking men from Ewell to give to Hill. Reasoning Ewell to be weakened, he prodded Warren and Sedgwick to try again and activated his reserves at Lacy House to hit Hill's left. This meant Wadsworth's division, having recovered from their earlier beating, would try to hit Hill in the flank.

Henry Heth was a solid division leader, but he was unable to knock Hancock's men off the Brock Road. He would later have his horse killed underneath him at Spotsylvania. (Library of Congress)

Union Major-General Wadsworth, earlier thrown back, tried once again, this time on A. P. Hill's flank, but darkness shut down the attack as seen in this print from an Albert Waud drawing. (Library of Congress)

By 6.30pm, Wilcox's men were in place and just in time, as Barlow began his attack. With no Longstreet and no darkness, the Rebels could only pray and hang on. Barlow smashed into the Rebel right, capturing nearly an entire regiment of North Carolina troops. Lee also misread developments, believing Grant had thrown most of his force against Hill, giving Ewell a chance. He urged the bird-like corps commander to attack.

Both sides were really too exhausted for any further serious action. The Union's inability to coordinate action in the dense woods had saved the Southern cause for the time being. Even Meade's attempt at 6pm to end-run Ewell's flank fell apart. All night skirmishers shattered the night with rifle fire. The dead and wounded littered the woods, the latter's pitiful cries mingling with screams coming from the surgeon's tents as amputated arms and legs piled up from their work.

It was time to assess the day's implications. Warren sat gloomily rewriting casualty reports to hide the carnage on his front. Sedgwick set to work getting his command in order, knowing that tomorrow would bring renewed fighting. Meade sent out orders intimating the same around 8pm. Grant gave voice to his frustration, directing Meade to coordinate a massive assault along the whole line no later than 6am. He was careful to make sure Burnside knew his role, since his corps basically sat on their hands in easy reach of the battlefield.

His army now assembled, Grant felt that he could crush Lee. Things had been sloppy on the 5th but on the 6th all would be different. He believed the mistakes were fixed, his corps were in order and a plan was in place to bring overwhelming numbers to bear, Longstreet or no Longstreet.

Lee was pondering the same problem. He wanted Longstreet to flank Hancock, but Hill was so pressed that he decided that Longstreet should backstop Hill. He sent an aide south who found the I Corps commander at Richard's Shop around 4pm. His men were exhausted after their long march and were flopping down where they stopped, too tired to pitch tents. Behind them were 32 miles with 10 more to go. Longstreet promised to resume the march at 1am.

Hopeful about Longstreet's arrival, Lee continued to urge Ewell to attack and the one-legged general was happy to oblige – two brigades would be launched against Sedgwick's entire corps. Meanwhile, he improved his earthworks in case the next morning's attack was repulsed. Hill's front was in tatters. Heth's and Wilcox's divisions were mixed together in a broken line with wide-open flanks. Both generals appealed to Hill for a withdrawal, but the ill corps commander assured them Longstreet was coming and to let the men sleep.

MAY 6 – DAY TWO OF THE BATTLE

True to his word, Longstreet began his march at 1am on May 6, Brigadier-General Joseph Kershaw's division going first, followed by that of Major-General Charles Field, the artillery under Brigadier-General Edward Porter Alexander bringing up the rear. His corps groped blindly to find their way through the poor roads and fields as daybreak drew ever closer. Lee and his anxious subordinates waited, but by first light, Old Pete's men could not be found. Hill's men knew they could not hold, but prepared to do their best.

Across the lines, Union soldiers stirred and assembled. At 5am, the signal was given and two columns formed and converged on the battered Rebel positions; Wadsworth's four brigades from the north and Hancock plus Getty straight down the Orange Plank Road, ten brigades strong.

Hill's eight brigades were in a fix. Behind them was the II Corps artillery by the Widow Tapp's Farm, but it was of little use against an enemy hidden by trees. A shout went up as Longstreet appeared, but died down with despair as men noticed he was without his corps. Hill's lines could take no more. They fought savagely, then retreated, threatening to unhinge the whole Confederate front. A flood of blue uniforms poured through the woods at their heels.

There was no sense of order to the retreat. Any attempt to stand was overwhelmed. Units in the rear not dug in were thrown back with the rest. Even a battery of guns positioned on the Orange Plank Road barely slowed the Yankee drive. Lee, watching from the Widow Tapp's field could only groan in misery as Hill's command slowly disintegrated before the Union onslaught.

In an hour, the entire Confederate right ceased to exist as a coordinated force. The coup de grace was to be delivered by Burnside, whose men had marched fast and idled long. The IX Corps commander carried out their deployment lackadaisically. Fuming, Hancock watched the momentum of his grand assault slowing for lack of fresh troops from Burnside. However, it was Hancock's surfeit of manpower that was working against him as the masses of men began getting in each other's way. The blue line paused to reorder their formations and begin what they thought would be the final charge to smash Hill.

Up by Widow Tapp's, the retreating Confederates streamed past a bewildered Lee. A. P. Hill, his stamina fading, ordered Lt. Col. William Poague's batteries to open fire, heedless that his own men were in the line of fire. Poague obeyed,

In this modern photo, two cannon and a caisson mark the position of the Confederate battery at Tapp Farm. In the distance, the Union troops would come pouring out of the woods. (Author's photograph)

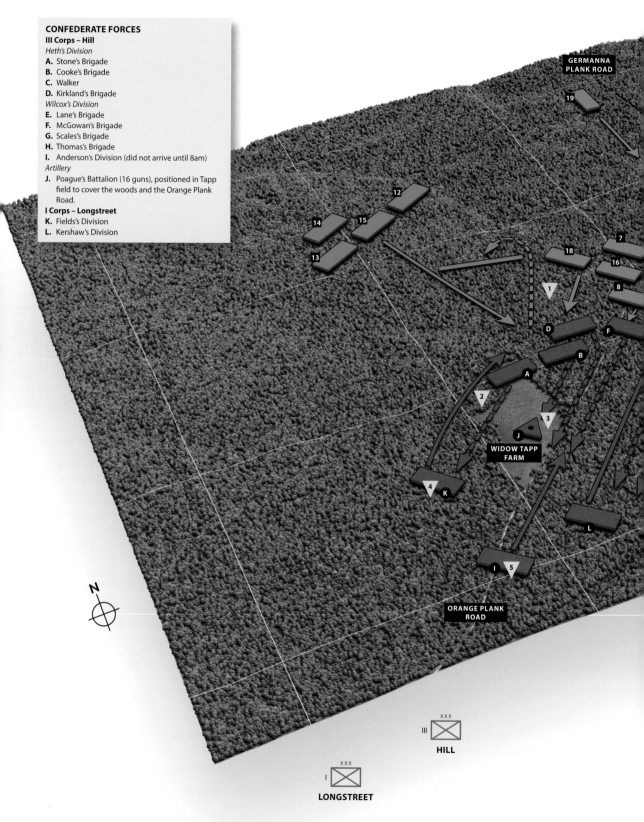

CONFEDERATE FORCES

III Corps – Hill

Heth's Division

A. Stone's Brigade

B. Cooke's Brigade

C. Walker

D. Kirkland's Brigade

Wilcox's Division

E. Lane's Brigade

F. McGowan's Brigade

G. Scales's Brigade

H. Thomas's Brigade

I. Anderson's Division (did not arrive until 8am)

Artillery

J. Poague's Battalion (16 guns), positioned in Tapp field to cover the woods and the Orange Plank Road.

I Corps – Longstreet

K. Fields's Division

L. Kershaw's Division

GERMANNA PLANK ROAD

WIDOW TAPP FARM

ORANGE PLANK ROAD

HILL

LONGSTREET

Note: Gridlines are shown at intervals of 1km

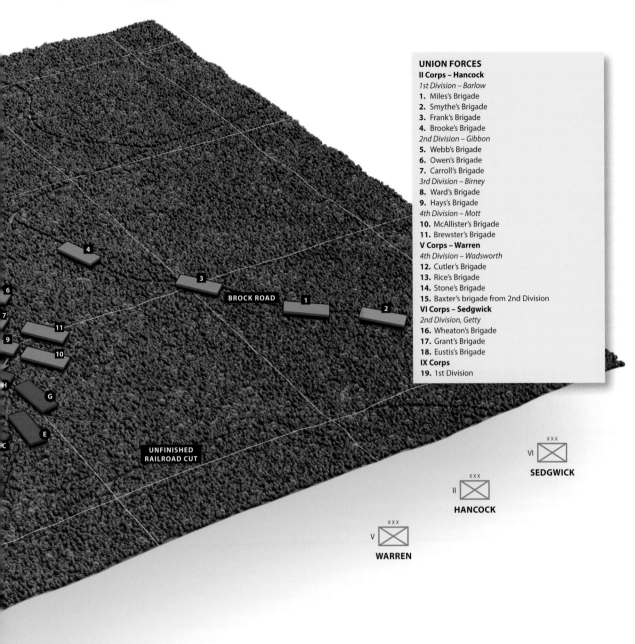

UNION FORCES

II Corps – Hancock
1st Division – Barlow
1. Miles's Brigade
2. Smythe's Brigade
3. Frank's Brigade
4. Brooke's Brigade
2nd Division – Gibbon
5. Webb's Brigade
6. Owen's Brigade
7. Carroll's Brigade
3rd Division – Birney
8. Ward's Brigade
9. Hays's Brigade
4th Division – Mott
10. McAllister's Brigade
11. Brewster's Brigade

V Corps – Warren
4th Division – Wadsworth
12. Cutler's Brigade
13. Rice's Brigade
14. Stone's Brigade
15. Baxter's brigade from 2nd Division

VI Corps – Sedgwick
2nd Division, Getty
16. Wheaton's Brigade
17. Grant's Brigade
18. Eustis's Brigade

IX Corps
19. 1st Division

BROCK ROAD

UNFINISHED RAILROAD CUT

XXX
VI [X]
SEDGWICK

XXX
II [X]
HANCOCK

XXX
V [X]
WARREN

EVENTS

1. 5.00am: Hancock forms two wings, one consisting of three of his divisions (minus Barlow, holding the Union left along Brock Road), and another using Wadsworth's division from Warren's V Corps. His main thrust attacks westward along the Orange Plank Road into Hill's exhausted two divisions.

2. 5.30am: both wings of the Union attack hit the Confederate line. Hill's men are little able to resist due to the spotty nature of their hasty entrenchments and exhaustion. One by one, the brigades fall back, whether they make a stand or are overwhelmed.

3. 6.00am: with the Confederate line in disarray, Hill orders the 12 guns of Poague's artillery battalion to fire across the Orange Plank Road from the field on the Tapp Farm, even though some of their own men are in the target area. Poague buys valuable time.

4. 6.00am: Longstreet's two divisions arrive and he masses them just out of sight behind the Tapp Farm. The Union attack has slowed due to the disorganization in their ranks and Longstreet prepares to counterattack. He sends in Gregg's Texas brigade to hold off the Union troops approaching Lee's headquarters at the Tapp farm and they hold for 20 minutes, losing half their number. Longstreet attacks in deep columns and stops the Union attack, pushing them back to the Confederate trench lines.

5. 8.00am: Anderson's division arrives and is placed under Longstreet. Longstreet conceives a plan to flank the Union line using an unfinished railroad cut to have his men march unseen to the flank. He spends the next two hours stabilizing his front, pushing back the Union line until he has a good defensive position to launch a counterattack against the Union left.

HANCOCK'S ATTACK ON HILL'S POSITION AND LONGSTREET'S RIPOSTE, 5.30AM, MAY 6, 1864

Hancock's II Corps, with help from units of Warren's V Corps, attacks the Confederate III Corps trench line.

12 field pieces holding off an entire corps, at least for now. His gunners could not stop the Yankees creeping around the flanks. It was looking very bad for the Confederate position.

Lee and Hill rode back and forth, trying to stem the gray rush. Porter Alexander mentions an interview with Brigadier-General Samuel McGowan from Wilcox's division. He recounted Lee riding up and saying, "My God, General McGowan, is this splendid brigade of yours running like a flock of geese?" McGowan replied, "No, General! The men are not whipped! They just want a place to form and they are ready to fight as well as ever."

Alexander was coming forward in the vanguard of Longstreet's corps and came across an excited officer on horseback trying to turn the tide. One of the officers with Alexander inquired, "Major, what's the matter? Are these men being marched back?" The enraged officer swore hotly, "No, God damn 'em! They are running!" It was at this point that several things happened that changed the fortunes of the day. Longstreet's men arrived.

His divisions jammed themselves down the Orange Plank Road, passing grisly reminders of the previous day's action stacked by Parker's Store. Cheers went up as Lee's "War Horse" thundered into view, dusty gray ranks behind him. They marched through Hill's broken soldiers as if on parade. Kershaw deployed his division as if the men were fresh and counterattacked north of the Orange Plank Road. Fields, given similar orders, lined his men up just behind Poague's artillery at the Tapp Farm.

Close to Lee's position was Brigadier-General John Gregg's Texans, a tough, veteran brigade. Gregg was part of Longstreet's corps, but Lee did not know him, and rode over to the unit as it marched forward. He looked at the grim faces and asked, "Whose boys are you?"

"Texas boys!" they shouted back.

"I am glad to see it," Lee replied. "Texans always move them!"

With a hearty "Hurrah for Texas!" Lee waved his hat and, caught up in the moment, rode along with them. Suddenly, the whole brigade stopped dead when they realized the beloved Lee was riding into danger as bullets pinged around them. They began to pluck at his reins, openly weeping and calling for him to turn back. "We won't go on unless you go back!" they shouted, but it took Gregg's pointing out to Lee that Longstreet had arrived and Lee had not conferred with him to stop what might have been death for the commander of the Army of Northern Virginia. Lee rode back and the Texans marched toward their blue antagonists, losing half their number according to Alexander.

Longstreet sorted out his two divisions with his usual skill and sent them each forward on a three-brigade frontage. Enraged at the thought of Lee being killed and eager to avenge Hill, they

Brigadier-General John Gregg's Texans marched across this field to clash with the Union troops, but only after they persuaded Lee not to lead them. Half of them never marched back. (Author's photograph)

slammed into Hancock's and Warren's men. The Union soldiers, still feeling victorious, knocked down the first line of assault but the next wave rushed over their fallen fellows, screaming at the top of their lungs. Now it was the Union turn to step back as their great masses were being torn up by accurate Rebel fire.

Fields, stopped after stunning Wadsworth, struggled to reorganize and continue attacking. Kershaw plowed on, straight into Mott and Birney. The gray troops blazed away, wilting the Federals like a furnace blast. They tumbled against Hancock's second line, hitting Getty's remaining brigade and wounding Getty. Still, the Yankees held on to a high spot as murderous fire erupted all around them. Kershaw personally led a charge, straightening his line as more Yankees began to pile in to help Getty's lone brigade. By 8am the battle reached a temporary balance. Both sides were combing the rear for reserve units to throw in.

Richard Anderson's division arrived after its masking position on the Rapidan was no longer needed, and, though it belonged to Hill, was given to Longstreet who held it in reserve. Hancock found Meade husbanding one of Burnside's divisions, but his superior would not release it unless there was an emergency. Hill dug in and made sure he held a contiguous line, managing to snatch back one of Anderson's brigades to bolster his line. Even Lee was deferring to Longstreet, clearly the savior of the army that day.

Along the Orange Turnpike, Warren's corps prepared to renew the offensive on their end. Warren worried about the gap between his corps and Hancock's but was assured that Burnside's corps would move up to the Chewning Farm.

Sedgwick, north of Warren, was concerned he would be on the defensive rather than attack at 5am as ordered. His men reported ominous sounds from the woods. Uneasy, "Uncle John" was convinced Ewell was up to no good. His fears proved to be correct as Rebels suddenly emerged from the dense woods. It turned out to be fruitless as Sedgwick's men handily threw them back and went in after them, only to be stopped dead as the Rebels jumped behind their earthworks and turned the gap between positions into a killing ground. Sedgwick's men could make no headway, even with superior numbers, and the casualties soared.

American artist Edwin Forbes sketched this panorama of the Wilderness battle. The building on the left is the Wilderness Tavern and the small building to the right of the center is Lacy House (also known as Ellwood), Warren's headquarters. Lined up on the right side are supply wagons, while ambulances clog the roads. The Orange Plank Road runs from bottom left to top right, crossed by the Germanna Road. To the left of the hill with Lacy House a line of troops march down Parker's Store Road. Forbes notes Hancock's corps is off the page to the left and a number of stragglers are in the foreground. (Library of Congress)

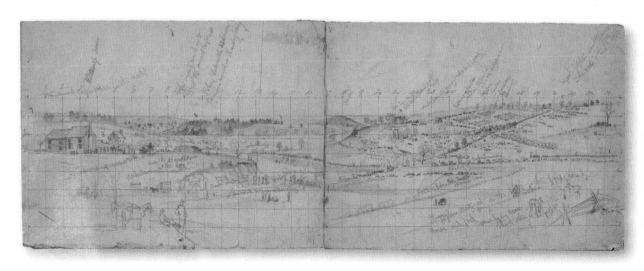

Warren, on hearing that Sedgwick was stymied, called off his attack, knowing his men would be crossing more open ground than VI Corps had. He needed one flank or the other to cave in. At 6am, he was still considering his options. Meade tried to shoo him along, but Warren came up with one excuse after the other to stay put. An hour later, Meade tried again, but Warren was concerned that Hancock was in trouble and continued to wait. Sedgwick, getting similar orders, tried again, but another bloody assault brought no breakthrough.

Meade gave up at that point. He had tried Grant's massive attack and Longstreet's arrival had undone the entire morning's offensive. A deadly stalemate ensued as both sides sniped and bombarded the opposing earthworks. Burnside's late arrival stopped any chance of recovering momentum after Longstreet's counterattack.

Burnside's orders were clear. He was to arrive at Wilderness Tavern by 4am. His first column did not arrive until 5am and the general himself did not show until 6am. Leaving one division in reserve, the whiskered Burnside sent his remaining two divisions toward the Chewning Farm to plug the gap in the Union line, but he shortly called a halt to rest and feed his worn troops. It was not until 7.30am that he got them moving again, and in a short time they came under fire.

Brigadier-General Robert Potter's 2nd Division ran into Stephen Ramseur's brigade from Rodes' division, thrown in to plug the Confederate gap. Alerted to Burnside's arrival, some of Hill's command slid sideways to connect with Ramseur. The door to flank Ewell was slammed shut in Burnside's face. IX Corps slid sideways itself, to the south and a connection with Wadsworth. Grant tried to get Burnside to coordinate with Hancock and crush the Confederate right, but lack of good maps hindered any decisive concerted action.

Instead, Meade scrambled to keep his line from being divided and defeated in detail. Both sides flung enormous amounts of bullets, piling up casualties to no avail. Union numbers were cut down by superior Confederate marksmanship.

By 9am, Hancock received a message that Sheridan was going to hit Longstreet along the Brock Road. This confirmed that Longstreet was flanking Hancock, causing him to worry about being hit from the south. Reports confirmed the appearance of the enemy, forcing Hancock to pull units out of line to extend his flank. While doing this, Hancock got another report that the Rebels were advancing as Wadsworth collapsed. Hancock thinned his line further to make contact with Warren. The morning's attack was over. It was Longstreet's turn.

In reality, only small numbers of Rebels had appeared on either front and friendly Union troops had been misidentified near the Brock Road. A brigade of cavalry under George Armstrong Custer ran into Rosser's horsemen. Custer's Michigan regiments, armed with repeating Spencer carbines, tore the attacking Rebels to shreds. Rosser refused to run and held on only with the help of artillery. This action became magnified in Hancock's mind and he was convinced George Pickett's Confederate division had joined Lee when it was miles away protecting Richmond.

Head-on attacks were making no headway. Both sides desperately searched for a way to outflank the other's lines. The Army of Northern Virginia's chief engineer, Major-General Martin Smith, was sent to

LONGSTREET'S TRIUMPH IS CUT SHORT BY HIS OWN MEN, 11AM, MAY 6, 1864 (PP. 50–51)

Lieutenant-General James Longstreet's day had been long and bloody. Starting before dawn, his men had marched straight down the Orange Plank Road and thrown themselves at Winfield Hancock's attacking Union II Corps, stopping them cold after the rout of Lt. Gen. A. P. Hill's III Confederate Corps. Longstreet was directing the entire Confederate right and he was looking for a way to drive back the Union troops. After learning of an unused railroad cut, he tasked Maj. Gen. Moxley Sorrel to use the cut to outflank Hancock's position on its left. The surprise was complete and Sorrel's four brigades smashed into the left flank so hard that Hancock later admitted to Longstreet that "you rolled me up like a wet blanket." Abandoned cook fires set the dry forest carpet alight and the Confederates charged on into flame and smoke.

Believing the attack needed more weight, the I Corps commander decided to head to the front himself, accompanied by a brigade of South Carolina troops under Brig. Gen. Micah Jenkins. Besides his staff, division commander Brig. Gen. Joseph Kershaw and Jenkins rode with Longstreet. Jenkins's brigade was dressed in brand-new uniforms of such a dark gray, one observer said they almost looked black. **(1)** Longstreet's aide worried that

the commander was too exposed riding in front of the brigade, to which Longstreet replied, "that is our business."

On the North side of the Orange Plank Road, Brig. Gen. William Mahone's 12th Virginia Regiment **(2)** was emerging from the woods and smoke to see some unknown troops in the brush on the other side of the road. Believing the dark uniforms to be Union blue, the Virginians opened fire, their color bearer coming forward to show the regimental flag. As he did, Jenkins' men released a volley in return, using a wide variety of rifled muskets typical of the Confederate supply situation. A man in the foreground hastily reloads, biting off the top of his paper cartridge to dump powder into his musket barrel before ramming home a .58-caliber Minié ball. **(3)**

Longstreet's party came riding into this crossfire. Kershaw turned to Jenkins' men yelling "They are friends!" but it was too late. Jenkins was shot through the skull. **(4)** Longstreet came forward to assist Kershaw when a bullet tore into his neck and exited out his right shoulder **(5)**. He was helped from his horse and later carried away, still urging his men to press on. He lived; Jenkins died.

order to attack. They were discovered by Rebels around 2pm, who went to greet them. The mass of blue infantry hit them at the same time, driving the Confederates back to their hastily constructed breastworks. Blasted by enemy fire as they tried to take the emplacements, Potter again fell back with the Rebels once again moving forward, but Burnside threw in a fresh brigade to stymie them and things settled down.

Grant urged Meade to have Burnside and Hancock attack simultaneously at 6pm after a suitable rest. Lee, however, was in no mood to wait. On word that Hill's and Anderson's corps were ready, he ordered them into a two-division assault straight down the Orange Plank Road at Hancock. They bounced off that strong position in a savage charge, broken by 12 pieces of artillery and protected Union defenders.

The Federal line seemed invincible until a fire broke out in some brush near Hancock's line, forcing it to be abandoned south of the Orange Plank Road. Confederates slammed into the breach, some rushing directly through the flames, to be mown down by case shot from Union cannon, but they kept coming, howling and firing. Double-loaded canister kept them from unhinging this line until more soldiers in blue could be brought in to counterattack and restore the line. They were in no shape to do much else, so, regardless of Grant's wishes, Hancock was done for the day.

Not so Burnside. He waded into Anderson's flank, throwing two divisions against the tired Rebels, forcing them back until fresh troops could countercharge and drive Burnside's men back to their entrenchments.

This photo shows Hancock and three of his division leaders, from left: Francis Barlow, Hancock (seated), David Birney and John Gibbon. Their actions up to May 9 were not particularly helpful to their reputations, but they would get their chance two days later. (Library of Congress)

Satisfied, the Confederates went back to their own works and the two sides snarled at each other while regaining their energy.

Darkness fell on a second day of awful carnage. Dead and wounded were of all ranks. Thousands lay about the dense woods, many too badly wounded to get to safety. Their awful cries filtered out of the blackness.

However, there was still one more card to play in the Confederate deck. Lee had failed to destroy Hancock, but on the northern flank, there was that pugnacious ex-businessman from Alabama, John B. Gordon. Gordon was one of those generals who had a keen mind for tactics and the undying love of his men.

JOHN B. GORDON'S SURPRISE FLANK ATTACK ON THE UNION RIGHT FLANK, EVENING MAY 6, 1864 (PP. 54–55)

Confederate Brig. Gen. John B. Gordon tried all afternoon to get his plan to attack the Union Army's right flank approved. His scouts found a way to march around to the north of the Union position, held by brigades from the Union VI Corps. Gordon personally examined the position in the morning, and found only a thin screen of skirmishers guarding the Union right. He could not, however, convince his division commander, Jubal Early, of the benefits of such an attack and the commander of II Corps, Richard Ewell, was concerned about being cut off from the corps on his right, belonging to A. P. Hill. That situation cleared up around noon and Ewell visited with army commander Robert E. Lee, who approved Gordon's plan. Hooking along Flat Run, north of the Orange Turnpike, Gordon commanded three regiments. In the darkening afternoon, his men got to within 100 yards of the Union trench line where they could see the men cooking (1) with

their rifles stacked (2), some soldiers in their small, two-man "pup" tents made from a sheet of canvas that each man carried and put together later (3).

At roughly 7pm, Gordon (4) ordered his men to advance. They fired a volley and charged, screaming at the tops of their lungs. The Union soldiers, some asleep, were caught completely by surprise. The flanking guards were swept aside (5) and the howling Confederates proceeded to roll up the entire flank, destroying the Union brigades of Brigadier-Generals Truman Seymour and Alexander Shaler, capturing both officers (6). Lieutenant-General John Sedgwick was nearly captured himself but managed to rally enough troops to stop the Confederate advance. As darkness stopped further action, it was by a narrow margin that the Union supply line was not cut and the Army of the Potomac defeated.

Originally from Georgia, he moved to Alabama as part of his father's business and formed his own unit at the war's start. Moving on to the 6th Alabama, his star rose with each battle until by 1864 he was commanding a brigade of Georgians under Jubal Early.

The ramrod straight general was still feeling for the Yankee right flank. Cavalry support helped firm up his information that there would be an opportunity to hit the flank and cut their supply line. There are varying accounts of what happened next, the most self-serving written by Gordon himself. Gordon rode forward that morning to look at the area and what he saw pleased him greatly. The Union line north of the Spottswood Road was hanging in the air and its defenders seemed lax in their vigilance. Gordon spent time trying to convince Early, but the latter was dismissive of the idea during a meeting with Ewell. Gordon tried again later in the day, but Ewell, seeing the possibilities, would not cross Early and force the issue.

Early was worried about where Burnside was going to end up. Gordon could only fume and watch the sun creep across the sky. The interval was marked by the arrival of Brigadier-General Robert Johnston's North Carolina Brigade released from duty near Richmond. After 1pm, Gordon tried again, only to be told no for a third time. His superiors could not know that Sedgwick's line was thinned due to the needs down on Hancock's end. Had Early allowed Gordon his attack, it would have pressed Sedgwick so hard that Hancock may have lost that source of support to keep his line from totally being destroyed.

Ewell did a personal reconnaissance, but, delayed by having to visit Lee, he did not approve of Gordon's plan until 5.30pm. Gordon claimed to have been present at the meeting, but this was hotly disputed after his memoirs were published. Quietly, Gordon's men, supported by Johnston's North Carolina Brigade and Brigadier-General John Pegram's Virginia Brigade, stole around the slender Union flank. They moved into a deep ravine and emerged on to a field where they formed up.

To their immediate front was a battalion of New York artillery, rifles stacked and settling down for dinner. Even so, the stream of wounded men filing past the cook fires put a tint of unease over the bucolic scene. Suddenly, from the darkness came a horde of Confederates yelling at the tops of their lungs. The New Yorkers ran for it and one regiment after another shattered

John B. Gordon was a man of skill and determination, always ready for action, as seen by his ramrod straight pose in this portrait. He was itching to slam into the Union right flank after finding it woefully unprotected. (Library of Congress)

Time has softened the Union trenches out on their right flank where Gordon made his attack. They were lightly defended and many men were cooking or sleeping after a long day. (Author's photograph)

and fled. Two brigades ceased to exist and Gordon's men drove them like cattle, hardly needing to fire until the gray line rolled up against Thomas Neill's brigade from Getty's division.

Rebels were everywhere and it was only the presence of Sedgwick himself that kept more units from running. Ewell punished the blue line with artillery. The Yankees needed help or they would be forced to follow their brethren to the rear, Sedgwick or no Sedgwick. Two brigade commanders fell prisoner and the Union right was looking like a bigger disaster than the left.

Meade remained defiant and Grant knew the numbers. He was confident he could hold with this preponderance of men and he was right. The darkness and dense woods shut down the offensive so that Sedgwick's bending line could hold. Neill's men were pressed, one brigade against two, but they beat back charge after charge. One staff officer feared that Lee was blocking a retreat route and Grant lost his temper for the only time that day. "Oh, I am heartily tired of hearing about what Lee is going to do! Some of you always seem to think he is suddenly going to turn a double somersault and land in our rear and on both flanks at the same time. Go back to your command and try to think what we are going to do ourselves, instead of what Lee is going to do."

This modern photo shows the point where Gordon attacked and nearly wrecked Sedgwick's corps. Only the personal intervention of Sedgwick himself prevented a disaster. Gordon had to satisfy himself with the destruction of two Union brigades and the capture of their commanders. (Author's photograph)

Grant and Meade funneled in reinforcements as Sedgwick strengthened his line. A second assault at 10pm was bloodily repulsed. Grant, who had

The race to Spotsylvania, May 7–8

1. The Union V Corps (Warren) departs after dark on May 7, 8.20pm, heading down the Orange Turnpike to Brock Road and turning south towards Todd's Tavern. His men file past the Tavern but are held up by Union cavalry blocking the road around 2.30am and have to push back enemy cavalry around 8am on the 8th.

2. The Union VI Corps (Sedgwick) moves off down the Orange Turnpike once Warren is out of the way and is instructed to turn toward Alrich from Chancellorsville and head past Piney Branch Church toward Spotsylvania. He leaves at 2.30am on the 8th, arrives at Chancellorsville around 4.30am, but his lead units do not arrive in the Laurel Hill area until 10.30am.

3. The Confederate I Corps (now under Anderson), alerted by Lee, leaves their entrenchments around 11pm on the 7th and heads down a road cut through the forest for them, arriving at Corbin's Bridge around 1am on the 8th. They stop after dawn at Block House Bridge.

4. The Confederate II Corps (Ewell) is ordered to leave around 1am on the 8th and proceeds to Parker's Store, then south to the Catharpin Road, turning east at that intersection and going down Shady Grove Church Road, where his corps arrives just before 1pm on the 8th.

5. The Union IX Corps (Burnside) was ordered to Chancellorsville and did not leave until 8am on the 8th. Once there, his corps marches to Alrich with the intention of heading to Piney Branch Church.

6. The Union II Corps (Hancock), leaves the Wilderness last of all Union units in order to guard the rear and flank of Grant's advance. His corps depart their position at daylight and follow Warren, stopping at Todd's Tavern.

7. The Confederate III Corps (Hill was replaced by Early in transit), is left to watch the Union positions and does not leave the Wilderness until mid-afternoon on the 8th and does not advance much farther than Corbin's Bridge until early on the 9th.

whittled enough sticks to wear holes in his gloves to maintain his calm, smoked a personal record of 20 cigars that day. Once the danger was over, he went to his cot and slept. The crisis passed. The Union commander of the Army of the Potomac beat his head against Lee for two days with little result and came near to having his army routed if not for the indecision and lack of coordination among Lee's subordinates. Clearly a new plan was needed. Grant had underestimated Lee's tactical skill and Lee had underestimated Grant's tenacity.

Grant was probably the first general officer to rise, with his next move already churning in his brain. In two days, Lee had inflicted 17,000 casualties on the Union Army for no gain. Grant refused to retreat, but the sounds coming from Confederate lines indicated they were digging in deeper. It was time to maneuver, so Grant devised a hooking march with one column heading down the Brock Road to Spotsylvania Courthouse, 10 miles away in more open terrain. The second column would go to Chancellorsville then loop back toward the crossroads where Grant hoped to force Lee to fight or retreat to Richmond. His note to Meade was time stamped 6.30am and said tersely: "General, make all preparations during the day for a night march to take position at Spotsylvania Courthouse."

Lee, while stopping Grant, could not claim victory. His losses were severe, nearly 11,000 by some estimates. He did not feel he could attack, but if Grant continued his push through the Wilderness, he believed he could blunt every thrust. He would need to keep his manpower up to stop Grant cold. Richmond, fearful of the armies closing in from the James and down the Shenandoah Valley, had little to offer.

Lee's army had let several opportunities pass. Lee, as commander, bears the final responsibility, but his corps commanders let him down for the most part and the man who could have driven off Hancock in a second Chancellorsville, like the late "Stonewall" Jackson, was struck down at the moment of triumph. Hill's illness, likely prostatitis, was making him unfit to command. He asked to be relieved and was replaced by Jubal Early.

Grant began to move during the night of May 7, hoping to sneak away before Lee had a chance to attack him while he was vulnerable. If he could beat Lee to Spotsylvania, he might be able to drive directly to Richmond without Lee holding him up. Lee would be the attacker then, with a depleted army. Ten miles down the road would tell the tale.

MAY 7–8 – THE RACE TO SPOTSYLVANIA

Grant's urgency was two-fold. One, he wanted to find Lee for a decisive battle and two, he did not want Lee to detach forces and crush Butler, who was in possession of City Point, a key location for assaulting Richmond. Late on May 7, his army began its ordered march. V Corps would head down the Brock Road followed by Hancock's II Corps. VI Corps and IX Corps were to head to Chancellorsville and then turn to Spotsylvania. Grant moved all the wagons and ambulances to Chancellorsville at 4pm, followed by the artillery reserve at 7pm. Around 8.30pm the infantry would march, starting with Warren's V Corps. II Corps would leave last, guarding the flank as the rest of the army moved.

Grant sent Sheridan's cavalry out ahead earlier that day. They cleared the Todd's Tavern area, then Brigadier-General Wesley Merritt's and James

Wilson's divisions headed down Brock Road where they tangled with Major-General Wade Hampton's and Major-General Fitzhugh Lee's divisions not far down the road, the fight lasting until dark.

Meade and Grant positioned themselves to join the advance and were heartily cheered by V Corps troops as they rode past. Grant had to order their officers to quiet them down so they wouldn't tip off the Rebels. Here was a general who would not back down before Robert E. Lee. Instead of retreating across the Potomac, Grant was flanking Lee and continuing his march south.

The march was long as the men stumbled down the dark roads in the hot, dry night. The movement of tens of thousands threw a dense cloud of dust into the air, combining with smoke from the previous day's fires. Delays due to the placement of Grant's headquarters and the cavalry screen took more hours from Grant's timetable.

Men, once stopped, often fell asleep immediately and time was lost getting them moving again. Instead of a smooth advance, the Army of the Potomac maintained a jerky pace and it was daybreak before II Corps was able to take its position in the line of march. IX Corps was the last to leave, not taking the road to Chancellorsville until full daylight, passing through on its way to Alrich, where the soldiers saw many grim reminders of last year's battle from scattered bones to full skeletons.

Hearing the sounds of movement, the Confederates sensed another victory and gave out three choruses of the Rebel yell. Scouts reported to Lee that the enemy appeared to be on the road to Chancellorsville but others said the pontoon bridge over the Rapidan was pulled up. Then came word of Stuart's cavalry clashing with Sheridan's men at Todd's Tavern.

Lee found the reports confusing, and with no definitive information decided to move Richard Anderson's I Corps toward Spotsylvania to provide either a blocking force if Grant was moving south, or a flanking force if he was heading to Fredericksburg. He wanted Anderson moving by 3am, but Anderson started off at 11pm, arriving at Block House Bridge by dawn.

Grant's men cheered when he directed them on the road to Spotsylvania, not back to Fredericksburg, as seen in this drawing by Edwin Forbes. Grant had no intention of retreating, but was going to flank Lee if possible. (Library of Congress)

MAY 8 – THE BATTLE OF SPOTSYLVANIA BEGINS

Sheridan's commanders started to push down the roads of advance before dawn. Their carbines and numbers forced Stuart's two divisions down the Brock and Fredericksburg Roads, drawing closer to Spotsylvania. Merritt's slow headway against the Rebels was worrisome, so by 6am he was calling on Warren's V Corps for help. Warren's men were tired from the night march, but they rose and advanced, Robinson's division in the lead. It took two hours to clear the road and get to the intersection of Brock Road and Old Courthouse Road. Worse, Wilson's bluecoats were pressing Fitzhugh Lee down the Fredericksburg Road.

Cavalry leader James Wilson inexorably pushed the Confederate cavalry down the Fredericksburg Road, hoping to smash an opening to Spotsylvania, where Grant could get between Lee and Richmond, the Confederate capital. (Library of Congress)

Appeals went to Anderson for help. Going beyond his orders from Lee, the new I Corps commander could not let the cavalry be destroyed and the strategic intersection taken. Quickly he sent two of Kershaw's brigades, Colonel John Henagan's South Carolinians and Brigadier-General Ben Humphrey's Mississippians, to stabilize the Brock Road, along with an artillery brigade under Major John Haskell.

Good, but not good enough; Fitzhugh Lee needed to stop Wilson cold, so two more brigades went that way. Wilson was in Spotsylvania, preparing to hold on to the key that would unhinge the Army of Northern Virginia from Richmond when he got an order from Sheridan to retire. Anderson, happy for that flank to be quietening down, occupied the town and turned his attention to the blue tide of Warren's corps. He dug in on top of Laurel Hill and waited for Ewell's II Corps.

Warren re-formed a line at the base of Laurel Hill around 8.30am, expecting Sedgwick's VI Corps to come up on his left and Hancock on his right. He knew he had to knock the Confederates off the hill to take the crossroad, so he called on Brigadier-General Robinson's 2nd Division to attack.

Robinson only had one brigade up and it was worn from marching. He asked for a rest, to which Warren initially assented before changing his mind ten minutes later. Robinson pushed forward his 1st Brigade plus a Maryland regiment from 3rd Brigade, thinking he only faced cavalry. A ripple of musket fire from Henagan's brigade quickly showed him he was wrong, and drove his men back.

Warren harangued the 2nd and 3rd Brigades, with Robinson personally leading another assault. They got within 50 yards of the top when Robinson went down, a musket ball shattering his left knee. The Union assault fell apart after that with the 3rd Brigade's Colonel Andrew Denison hit in the right arm. Both men would lose their wounded limbs due to the nature of the low velocity soft Minie balls splintering the bones to irreparable ruin. All color bearers and officers of the Maryland regiment were hit. The momentum bled away and more Confederate reinforcements sent the remnants stumbling back down the hill.

Warren understood the urgency of the situation but not the condition of his men. He threw in a brigade from Griffin's division as it arrived, still thinking it was only cavalry at the top of Laurel Hill. That assault failed, as did one by the Iron Brigade. By 12.30pm, Warren realized he was up against the entire I Corps and asked for ammunition and reinforcements. Lee, meanwhile, directed Ewell to join Anderson while Grant, seeing the situation looking like a counterattack, sent Sedgwick and Burnside to join Warren.

Sedgwick's men started arriving from 10.30am, but it was 5pm before he was formed up. This allowed Ewell to arrive and move behind Anderson to a spot east of the Brock Road. At 6pm, another attack started, but it was hastily organized and went forward in a disjointed fashion. A determined counterattack by Brigadier-General Stephen Ramseur's and Brigadier-General Cullen Battles' brigades from Rodes' division was stopped by the growing dark. The Union opportunity to flank Lee failed. Grant got no result except 1,500 more casualties.

This colorful Kurz and Allison print shows the Union assault on Laurel Hill, where they found Confederate infantry dug in. Grant lost over 1,000 men trying to take the hill. (Library of Congress)

MAY 9 – LEE DIGS IN

Warren's repulse and Sheridan's failure to push out the Rebel cavalry gave Lee what he needed – time to form a line. All three of his corps filed into the Spotsylvania area and began to throw up extensive fieldworks. Meade and Sheridan got into an awful row when the latter showed up at Meade's headquarters. Meade accused Sheridan of incompetence, stinging Sheridan's pride so that he threw down a bold claim – that he could whip Jeb Stuart.

Meade went to see Grant and have Sheridan punished. Most of it went in one of Grant's ears and out the other except for the part about whipping Stuart. Grant ordered Meade to send Sheridan off to make good on his claim. This had unforeseen consequences, not the least of which was depriving the army of scouting reports. Burnside's IX Corps moved slowly forward and by 3am on the 9th it was blocked by Sheridan's cavalry corps preparing to take on Stuart. It took hours to clear the road, putting Burnside on the banks of the Ny around 7am but no further, being held up by a pugnacious Rebel line.

Trying to attack down the Fredericksburg Road wasn't where Grant wanted him anyway, so he stretched out toward the rest of the army, to the right of his current location. Hancock marched through Todd's Tavern on the 8th and got into a small engagement with Jubal Early's III Corps. It died down as Early rushed off to Spotsylvania and Hancock resumed marching the following morning, coming along the Brock Road to sit alongside V Corps' right, digging into the high ground near the Po River.

Warren and Sedgwick spent the 9th improving their positions. Brigadier-General Gershom Mott's 4th Division of II Corps was sent to fill a gap to the left of VI Corps while IX Corps approached. Meanwhile the irascible Meade punished Warren over the failure to take Laurel Hill by putting Sedgwick in charge of him. Sedgwick ignored the order.

The entrenching on both sides continued into the 9th, with Ewell's corps moving into an odd-shaped semi-circle north of the Brock Road. Early remained at Spotsylvania Courthouse to fend off Burnside. Snipers were active on both sides and the Union got the worst of it during these exchanges.

Sedgwick was in a good humor that morning. To inspect his positions, he walked the skirmish line, making fun of a soldier who dodged a bullet. After an exchange with the soldier, the bearded Sedgwick declared that the Confederate snipers "couldn't hit an elephant at this distance!" Sadly, a fellow with a Whitworth rifle got a look at Sedgwick and began to bang away. His third shot struck the smiling general in the face, spinning him around. His staff officer,

Laurel Hill as it appears today. The waving grasses were trampled and covered with corpses as Lee held this position against two Union corps. (Author's photograph)

Lieutenant-Colonel Martin McMahon, tried to catch him, but both men fell to the ground, Sedgwick still smiling, even in death. Patrols tried to exact revenge, but the snipers slunk away, their murderous job done.

Grant was so shocked he inquired twice to make sure, saying, "his loss to the army is greater than the loss of a whole division of troops." Sedgwick was an excellent general, and command now fell to Brigadier-General Horatio G. Wright, commander of the 1st Division of Sedgwick's corps. Brigadier-General David A. Russell of Wright's 3rd Brigade succeeded Wright as 1st Division commander. The next day, the IX Corps' 1st Division commander, Brigadier-General Thomas G. Stevenson, fell as a bullet blew off the back of his head while conferring with staff. Colonel David Leasure of Stevenson's 2nd Brigade replaced him, since Burnside had no other available general to put in the spot.

The two armies slowly consolidated their positions. Hancock's three remaining divisions lined up to Warren's right along the Po River with Warren still at the foot of Laurel Hill, while Wright's (ex-Sedgwick's) corps was between the Brock Road and a stream, Mott's division near the Brown Farm and Burnside across the Ny at the Fredericksburg Road.

Early had one division (Mahone's) to the left of Anderson near where the Po River crossed Shady Grove Church Road. Anderson stretched from there to where the Brock Road split the line. Ewell's entire corps occupied the half-oval of a salient over half a mile long on high ground that Lee could not afford to give up due to its command of the area. In all, the lines stretched nearly 7 miles.

Jubal Early was a tough scrapper and put his corps into the line against Burnside's IX Corps. (Library of Congress)

This Waud sketch shows the section of line where John Sedgwick was killed by a sniper. Note the log walls meant to ward off enemy bullets and the scenes of soldiers trying to rest or have a smoke while waiting for the next assault. (Library of Congress)

This modern photo shows Warren's position at the bottom of Laurel Hill. The trees in the photo would have been cut down to make breastworks in 1864. (Author's photograph)

Both sides dug in along those lines, throwing up man-high breastworks covered with earth excavated from trenches behind them. The Confederate defense lines were overseen by Lee's chief engineer, who made sure that the approaches were covered with arcs of supporting fire and sited cannon in hastily dug lunettes, so that any Union assault would be savaged from the start.

Grant, initially unwilling to send his men against the growing line of trenches and abatis, was buoyed by a number of reports that indicated the Confederates had vanished from their skirmish positions around Todd's Tavern but were apparently attacking Brigadier-General Orlando Willcox's 3rd Division of Burnside's corps. He assumed that Lee was loading up his right flank against Burnside.

This gave him the idea to send Hancock's corps to flank the Confederate left, reasoning it to be weaker. The other good news was a report from Benjamin Butler's command. Butler had landed at City Point in Virginia and was marching on Petersburg, a critical rail junction near Richmond. Hancock moved off mid-afternoon on the 9th.

Edwin Forbes' drawing shows the center of the Union line around May 9. He put in a list of notes for the engravers. The number 2 denoted the Union breastworks closest to the enemy. Other notes showed caissons, stacks of arms, men shielded by piles of wood and a battery of cannon facing the enemy. (Library of Congress)

He promptly ran into trouble. It was terrain trouble, though. He was going to cross the Po and advance to Shady Grove Church Road, then turn left to get around the Rebel left flank where the Po bent south. The land was uneven and dense and it was 6pm before his men crossed the Po where it ran east to west, using pontoon bridges. They found the road, but dense woods slowed Hancock's advance to the north–south bend of the river and darkness shut him down.

He called it quits around 8pm and Grant did not disagree. His movement, however, caused Lee a great deal of consternation, so much so that he called on Jubal Early to send Brigadier-General William Mahone's division to Block House Bridge Road and then asked Early for Major-General Henry Heth's division to shore up the same position, leaving Major-General Cadmus Wilcox's lone division to watch Burnside as day dawned on May 10th.

MAY 10 – UPTON'S NEAR-TRIUMPH

Grant was frustrated with Lee beating him to the punch and the limitations of his commanders to unhinge the Confederate line before they turned it into a formidable defensive position. He wanted action and tried to work around the situation. His nature would not let him sit still and bombard a static line.

Meanwhile, Hancock was still trying to cross the Po and strike the Rebel positions, but he was stymied by Mahone's arrival at Block House Bridge. He cast around for another way. Future Native American fighter and Spanish–American War leader Nelson A. Miles from Barlow's division pushed a regiment downstream, but got tangled with Rebel skirmishers.

Grant ordered Hancock to give it up, leave Barlow's division to deal with Mahone, and send two other divisions toward Warren and join in a general assault around 5pm. Wright's VI Corps plus the attached II Corps division of Mott would attack the west side of the Confederate salient and Burnside would try to march on Spotsylvania Court House. He was certain Lee had to be weak somewhere, so an attack at all points should find a point to crack, at least in theory.

Nelson Miles' attempt to flank the Rebel line along the Po was stymied by well-hidden enemy skirmishers. He would go on to fame in the Spanish–American War. (Library of Congress)

The battle of Spotsylvania, May 8–11

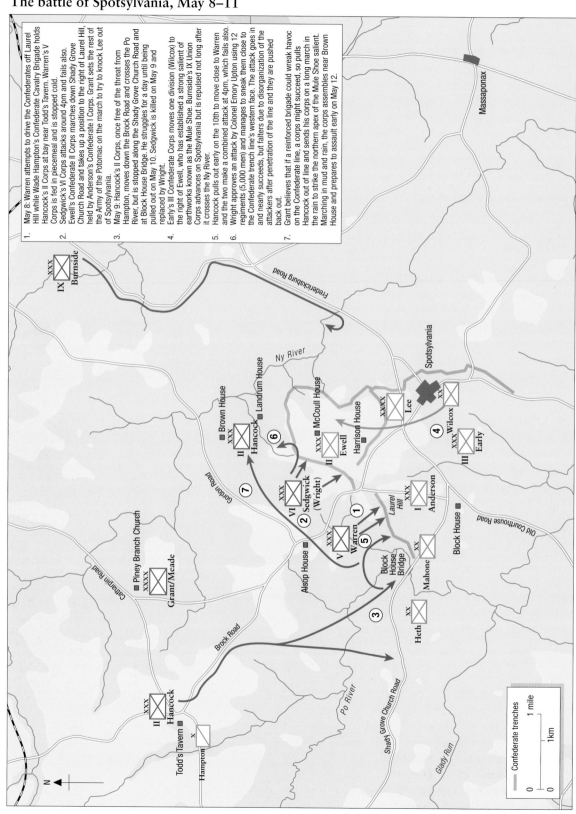

1. May 8: Warren attempts to drive the Confederates off Laurel Hill while Wade Hampton's Confederate Cavalry Brigade holds Hancock's II Corps at bay near Todd's Tavern. Warren's V Corps is fed in piecemeal and is stopped cold.

2. Sedgwick's VI Corps attacks around 4pm and fails also. Ewell's Confederate II Corps marches down Shady Grove Church Road and takes up a position to the right of Laurel Hill, held by Anderson's Confederate I Corps. Grant sets the rest of the Army of the Potomac on the march to try to knock Lee out of Spotsylvania.

3. May 9: Hancock's II Corps, once free of the threat from Hampton, moves down the Brock Road and crosses the Po River, but is stopped along the Shady Grove Church Road and at Block House Bridge. He struggles for a day until being pulled out on May 10. Sedgwick is killed on May 9 and replaced by Wright.

4. Early's III Confederate Corps moves one division (Wilcox) to the right of Ewell, who has established a strong salient of earthworks known as the Mule Shoe. Burnside's IX Union Corps advances on Spotsylvania but is repulsed not long after it crosses the Ny River.

5. Hancock pulls out early on the 10th to move close to Warren and the two make a combined attack at 4pm, which fails also. Wright approves an attack by Colonel Emory Upton using 12 regiments (5,000 men) and manages to sneak them close to the Confederate trench line's western face. The attack goes in and nearly succeeds, but falters due to disorganization of the attackers after penetration of the line and they are pushed back out.

6.

7. Grant believes that if a reinforced brigade could wreak havoc on the Confederate line, a corps might succeed, so pulls Hancock out of line and sends his corps on a long march in the rain to strike the northern apex of the Mule Shoe salient. Marching in mud and rain, the corps assembles near Brown House and prepares to assault early on May 12.

Confederate trenches

0   1 mile

0   1km

Hancock spent the day organizing his march to satisfy Grant. Barlow had some difficulty extricating himself from his position near Block House Bridge due to enemy fire, but the arrival of Birney's division helped him, as Heth's division smashed into him again and again. Barlow refused to yield as the bodies piled up but the ferocity of the Rebel attacks soon turned a retreat into a confused runaway as units broke and fled.

It was so bad that II Corps lost its first cannon in combat when a Rhode Island battery got one stuck between two trees and had to abandon it. Barlow managed to get away as the woods caught fire, slowing the Rebel advance. So, Hancock's loss was Heth's gain as he brought his line even with Mahone along the Shady Grove Church Road and advanced while II Corps units scampered back across the Po.

Meanwhile, Meade urged Warren to hit the salient and chose Gibbon's division from II Corps to start, with Warren committing Cutler and Crawford's divisions, putting Gibbon between them. However, his first problem was not the enemy but the uneven land gashed by a ravine and covered with dense undergrowth. Beyond that lay the Confederate works, the defenders protected by masses of logs and ringed by dead trees with limbs and roots sharpened and projecting like a phalanx of spears.

Brigadier-General Hobart Ward led his 1st Brigade from Birney's division to the muzzles of the Confederate guns before being driven back. (Library of Congress)

A little before 3pm, Warren was listening to reports of his men being pinned down as they approached the Confederate trenches. The men were tired and being picked off a few at a time. Warren decided to go ahead with the attack around 4pm, but his assault was little more than a mob's rush due to the thick woods. Cutler's division charged into a wall of flame from Law's brigade and was stopped cold. A second line tried to claw their way forward, but Brigadier-General James Rice of Cutler's 3rd Brigade fell mortally wounded and the first line broke, spilling back into the second line, sending them back as well. As one Pennsylvanian remarked, the attack was "no holiday task."

Crawford's division ran into Brigadier-General John Gregg's Texans, the same brigade that prevented Lee from leading them at the Wilderness. Crawford was stopped and so was Gibbon. The woods littered with their dead, three divisions trudged out of the dense vale to their positions.

Hancock, after seeing to a false alarm of an enemy attack, sent the same divisions back against the salient, along with Brigadier-General J. Hobart Ward's 1st Brigade from Birney's division of II Corps. Around 7pm, the men went forward with fear of death tugging at their hearts. They felt so with good reason. The Rebels were sending out patrols to collect extra ammo and weapons from the dead, calling out to the glum Yankees to come closer next time

so they wouldn't have to walk so far to load up. Well supplied, and some having extra muskets beside them, the Confederates opened up with a terrific and continuous volley of fire, including canister, mowing down the first attempt and setting the underbrush ablaze. A second attempt was driven back as well.

Hobart Ward's men, fresher than the rest, got a bit closer, marching almost to the cannon muzzles of G. T. Anderson's Georgians before breaking. It didn't all go Lee's way, though. One section of the line in front of part of Ward's men from the 3rd Maine and 86th New York, thinking the battle over, promptly started to cook dinner or fall asleep where they stood, including Colonel Robert Taylor. A mix of Gregg's and Anderson's men was caught off guard as the two Yankee regiments scrambled over the earthworks and jumped the exhausted men in gray. A hand-to-hand melee ensued with Taylor

ABOVE
Colonel Emory Upton led a 12-regiment assault on the Confederate position after a path through the woods allowed the Union forces to get close to the Rebel salient. (Library of Congress)

RIGHT
Forbes depicts the difficult situation the Union faced assaulting the Mule Shoe salient. The Union breastworks are in the foreground and the hapless Union soldiers have thrown themselves down in a depression while waiting to assault the enemy breastworks on the crest. (Library of Congress)

snatching up a hot frying pan and laying into both friend and foe, angry at having his meal interrupted. Canister finally drove the enemy back and that part of the attack sputtered out, costing 5,000 Union dead for no gain.

Wright pushed his corps on and was briefly buoyed by the discovery of a path through the woods to the enemy position by his 1st Division commander Brigadier-General David Russell. Russell's men finished clearing the woods of Rebel sharpshooters and he asked Wright to order a charge down the path, some 200 yards in length. Wright thought the request had merit and gathered 5,000 men from 12 regiments for the assault.

He put this mass of infantry under Colonel Emory Upton, who went with his subordinate commanders to survey the enemy line. It was large and daunting, a veritable fortress of logs backed by artillery ensconced in lunettes. Undeterred, Upton structured his force into four lines, three regiments wide. The first rank would approach with loaded muskets while the follow-up had fixed bayonets and they were forbidden to fit percussion caps to discourage them from losing momentum by stopping to fire at the enemy.

Upton laid out a very intricate plan for each line and each regiment in the line. A short bombardment would precede the assault. The attack was scheduled for 5pm but did not get off until 6pm. As the blue troops broke from the woods, the first line shouted almost in unison and climbed up the abatis, straight into Dole's brigade of Georgians from Ewell's corps.

As the first Yankees overtopped the fieldworks, Dole's men shot them down. The second line plunged into the midst of the enemy, tossing their bayonet-tipped muskets like javelins. Upton's plan was working. While the Georgians ducked flying weapons and struggled to reload, blue troops poured over the parapet, clubbing rebels or taking prisoners. More and more Federals swarmed over the logs, spreading left and right, sending defenders fleeing in all directions.

Once in, the assaulting columns saw another line of emplacements and rushed for them. The initial movements laid down by Upton dissipated in the violent scramble of the moment. It was time for more troops to arrive and solidify the gains. That would have been Gershom Mott's 4th Division from Hancock. Mott certainly had a tough row to hoe. First, he had to figure out whose orders he was supposed to obey. He was from I Corps, currently under VI Corps, and was required to maintain contact with Burnside's IX Corps.

This quick Waud sketch shows Upton on horseback in the midst of the charging Yankees as they pour over the Confederate breastworks. (Library of Congress)

Wright expected him to attack, but in order to stay in contact with Burnside, Mott was required to stretch out a skirmish line over 2 miles long. The day's business of maintaining that line took a physical toll on him and now he had orders to attack at 5pm.

Mott did his best, throwing up a bombardment from his divisional artillery and sending his men out on time (he never got the message about the delay) and watched as they suffered under enemy shelling during the 500-yard approach only to be turned back as the Rebels hit them with canister. Upton's help was gone.

Of course, there was Burnside, and of course he got his orders directly from Grant around 10.30am to attack. Grant's orders were a little vague, encouraging Burnside to do his best. Burnside was trying to do just that, over thinking his plans, and by 6pm, his attack turned into a half-hearted advance down the Fredericksburg Road to dig a trench line on Lee's flank close to the courthouse. Grant ordered him back as being too far from the main line and blamed himself for Burnside's inaction.

Lee's men, however, were prepared for a breach. As Upton's command began to fan out it was hit by Brigadier-General James Walker's brigade on its right while Colonel William Witcher's (ex-Jones) and Brigadier-General George Steuart's brigades moved in on the left. Ewell arrived and brought up several more units from the reserves. The Yankees were shoved back out, lost cannon were recovered and volleys from them kept the bluecoats moving along.

Out of reserves, Upton could not recover the initiative, barely holding on as the Rebels drove his men back. Upton failed to unravel the line but he sent over 1,000 hapless Confederates to Federal prisons. His own casualties were severe, with many officers among the 1,000 or so lost in the assault. The poor showing did not deter Grant. He calmly wired Halleck for more replacements and ammunition. He considered Upton's attack failed only because it wasn't big enough.

That night most action was confined to taking care of wounded and competition between the bands of both sides until both settled on "Home Sweet Home." The formidable Confederate salient was now dubbed "the Mule Shoe" and sounds of axes filtering out of the darkness were signs that the defenses were getting stronger. Unfazed, Grant reported that he would "fight it out on this line if it takes all summer," despite the loss of 20,000 men.

Major-General Gershom Mott's 4th Division of II Corps was stretched to the utmost trying to hold a long line and assault at the same time. Canister shredded his assault. (Library of Congress)

Grant was convinced that Lee's army was worn down and one good push would cause it to fall apart. He was buoyed by reports from the Richmond front as Butler was making some headway at Bermuda Hundred and Phil Sheridan was doing a Jeb Stuart in reverse, going behind Lee and leaving a trail of sabotage and destruction. The Northern press lauded Grant's pugnacious declaration and it looked like "Unconditional Surrender" Grant was poised to finish Lee.

On the 11th, Grant took time to sort out the situation for another try. He tried to find a weak spot in Lee's Mule Shoe salient and sent Meade around to canvass the corps commanders to see what shape they were in. The salient, jammed with enemy soldiers, seemed like the spot to hit and bag a lot of Rebels. Upton captured 1,000 with a brigade, maybe a corps this time, he thought.

Defensive lines were improved, supplies were topped off and the men rested, except for skirmishers. Grant issued his offensive plan at 3pm that day. He decided that Hancock's corps would deliver the main blow at the apex of the salient. That meant a night march to a position just north of the salient near the Brown House to the left of Warren's position.

Wright and Warren were to remain in close contact with the enemy and Hancock would begin with a two-division attack in conjunction with Burnside's IX Corps. Grant sent two aides to Burnside to "help" him see the importance of a vigorous offensive.

Lee was busy as well. Grant's orders to Sheridan were bearing fruit. Jeb Stuart went off in pursuit of the diminutive cavalry leader with over 4,000 troopers, only a third the size of Sheridan's command. For two days Stuart chased Sheridan as the latter burned tons of supplies and dozens of rail cars. Stuart tried to catch up and coordinate with friendly troops guarding Richmond, but Sheridan had such a head start that Stuart's men soon tired and had to rest the day Upton was making his assault.

Resuming his pursuit, Stuart got ahead of Sheridan the morning of the 11th. As Grant and Lee pondered the lessons of Upton's attack, Stuart threw back Sheridan's advance guard at Yellow Tavern on the Brock Turnpike just a few miles outside of Richmond. Sheridan piled two divisions into the attack. Charge and countercharge followed with Stuart leading a desperate attack that threw the Federals back.

The wild, swirling fight gave a Michigan trooper his chance. He recognized the flamboyant plume and

Members of the 1st Massachusetts Heavy Artillery were tasked with burying the dead. By May 10, the Union had suffered 20,000 casualties. (Library of Congress)

luxurious beard of Stuart and fired, striking Stuart in the chest. The Union men broke off and pushed around toward Richmond, where local forces turned them aside and forced them to seek safety behind Ben Butler's lines. Lee received the news with bitterness. "He never brought me a false piece of information," he remarked.

Stuart lingered until May 12, when, after singing a hymn with local clergy, the great cavalryman died at 5pm, one of thousands who fell that day. Lee's eyes, one could argue, were being blinded. His nephew Fitzhugh Lee assumed command. A solid soldier, he was no Jeb Stuart.

Visiting the Mule Shoe, Lee listened to his chief engineer about how improved the positions were, and his patrols could find no trace of enemy concentrations nearby. Digesting this, he shuffled Dole's battered brigade out of line and replaced it with Colonel William Monaghan's Louisiana Brigade. Heth's division was sent from the quiet Po front toward Spotsylvania Courthouse and Burnside's muddled thrust. Whether prescient or practical, Lee decided to drive a trench line across the base of the salient as a precaution.

Fitzhugh Lee, nephew of Robert E. Lee, assumed command of the Confederate cavalry of the Army of Northern Virginia upon the death of Jeb Stuart on May 12. He had huge shoes to fill. (University of Kentucky)

This contemporary photograph was taken at the tip of the Mule Shoe salient, showing the dense woods that the Union attackers had to navigate to get to the Confederate trenches during a thick fog. (Library of Congress)

Once full darkness was across the front, Hancock called together his commanders and let them know about the coming attack. Barlow and Birney left first, around 10pm. They tried to practice absolute silence and did not put out their cookfires. V and VI Corps men extended their lines to keep up the continuous front, assisted by gunners from Colonel J. Howard Kitching's Heavy Artillery Brigade, who filled some of the trenches left by Hancock.

The march was miserable. It was dark and the same rain which bogged down Sheridan drenched the tired, stumbling soldiers. Occasional noisy incidents kept the troops on edge, but in general, the march was a success and the units began to gather near Brown House. There the commanders tried to get a handle on the ground they were to march through.

From Brown House, Hancock's units would march south on a 400-yard

front through clearing and open fields as the ground rose toward the Mule Shoe. Gibbon pulled in around 3am and Barlow's and Mott's divisions would lead the attack, the other two held in reserve. The men lay on the soft, wet ground and tried to rest.

While Hancock and Burnside readied their attack forces, the restless Lee made a mistake that almost cost him his whole army. His remark that Stuart never gave him bad information came back to haunt him as he listened to a report from his own son, W. H. F. "Rooney" Lee, a major-general since April. The eager cavalry officer reported that the Yankees were moving their wagons to Fredericksburg and Burnside had abruptly countermarched back behind the Ny River.

Buoyed by this, Lee told Ewell that the Union Army was in retreat toward Fredericksburg and he wanted to catch them moving and try to cause them some harm. He then gave specific orders to get Ewell's corps artillery limbered up and ready to pursue. In all, ten pieces were pulled back to a road where they could move quickly. Ironically, Lee gave orders for Ewell's men to light no fires as they rested in the rainy weather, in anticipation of his own thrust.

Indications began to come in that such plans were premature. Men were reporting hearing the sounds of troops moving at the front of the Mule Shoe and spoke to George "Maryland" Steuart, who duly expressed his concerns to his divisional commander, Major-General Edward "Allegheny" Johnson. Johnson literally begged Ewell for the guns back. Ewell promised them by 2am, but they didn't even start moving until 3.30am. Sleepy men, confused orders and lack of deep reserves (only two brigades stood by in case of a breakthrough) were adding up to a disaster.

Here is part of the Confederate trench line along the Bloody Angle. Today it just seems like part of the landscape and not a formidable obstacle strewn with corpses from the May 12 assault. (Photo by Rich Allen)

MAY 12 – THE BLOODY ANGLE

The rain stopped and gave way to a thick fog. To the wet, tired men of Hancock's corps, it covered the attack path so thoroughly that they could not see where they were going. Hancock held off starting until a bit after 4.30am when the light was better. Upward into the disorienting whiteness went four divisions, two abreast.

Pickets were encountered, but the grim blue horde emerging from the mist sent them running off. Still, Hancock was forced to peel off half of Gibbon's men to guard the Union left flank. Once the parapets were in sight, the march turned into a disorderly rush forward in hopes of catching the defenders unaware. Obstructions some 100 yards from the main line were hastily thrown aside, but by now the enemy was growing aware and firing sporadically.

Birney's division plunged straight in, while Barlow's hit the tip of the salient and spread to get over to the east of McCoull House. Over the

This photo was taken of what a fellow visitor referred to me as the real part of the line where the Confederate artillery was captured on May 12. He believed that the semi-circular rise was a lunette dug for cannon, instead of where the sign marks the Bloody Angle. (Author's photograph)

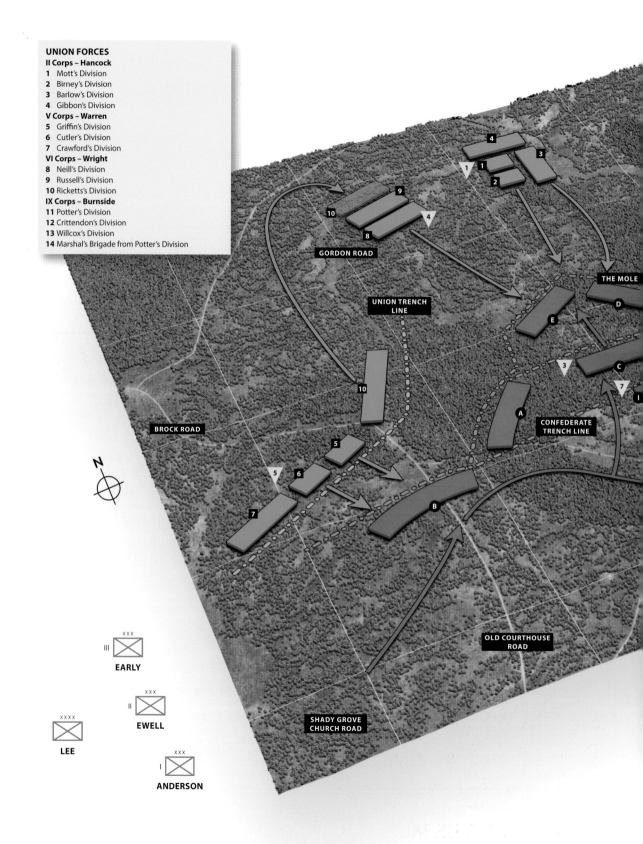

UNION FORCES

II Corps – Hancock
1 Mott's Division
2 Birney's Division
3 Barlow's Division
4 Gibbon's Division

V Corps – Warren
5 Griffin's Division
6 Cutler's Division
7 Crawford's Division

VI Corps – Wright
8 Neill's Division
9 Russell's Division
10 Ricketts's Division

IX Corps – Burnside
11 Potter's Division
12 Crittendon's Division
13 Willcox's Division
14 Marshal's Brigade from Potter's Division

GORDON ROAD

THE MOLE

D

E

UNION TRENCH LINE

C

CONFEDERATE TRENCH LINE

A

BROCK ROAD

B

N

OLD COURTHOUSE ROAD

III EARLY

II EWELL

SHADY GROVE CHURCH ROAD

LEE

ANDERSON

Note: Gridlines are shown at intervals of 1km

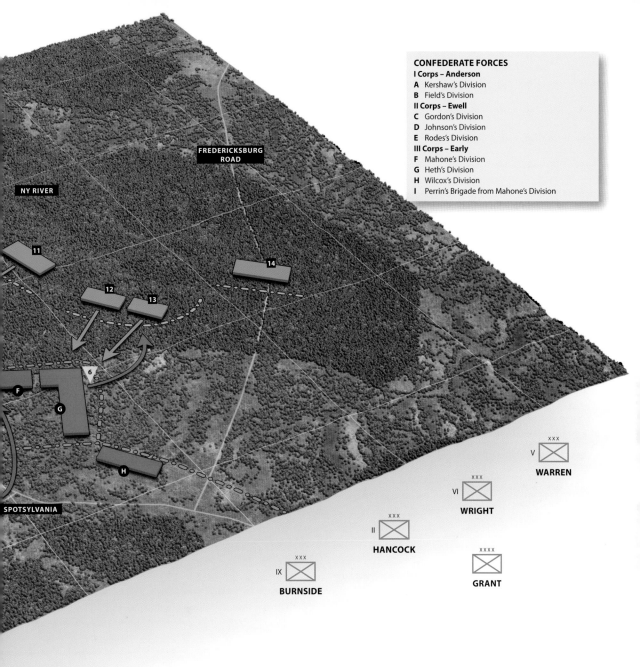

CONFEDERATE FORCES

I Corps – Anderson
A Kershaw's Division
B Field's Division
II Corps – Ewell
C Gordon's Division
D Johnson's Division
E Rodes's Division
III Corps – Early
F Mahone's Division
G Heth's Division
H Wilcox's Division
I Perrin's Brigade from Mahone's Division

FREDERICKSBURG ROAD

NY RIVER

SPOTSYLVANIA

V xxx WARREN

VI xxx WRIGHT

II xxx HANCOCK

IX xxx BURNSIDE

xxxx GRANT

▼ EVENTS

1. Three of Hancock's divisions (Gibbon is in reserve) line up by Brown House at 4.00am. Barlow's division is the Union left, while Birney is the Union right. Mott lines up behind Birney. At 4.30am they go forward in the dense fog, overcoming pickets until reaching the apex of the Mule Shoe salient. The Confederates are completely off guard, many asleep, and Johnson's division is swiftly overwhelmed. Thousands of prisoners and several cannon are captured, including Johnson himself. The assault mushrooms once over the wall and causes more and more Confederate units to rout or fall back in confusion.

2. Burnside assaults the east face of the salient, getting to the actual main line. All three of his divisions present attack, leaving only the Provisional Brigade from Potter's division to hold the road to Fredericksburg.

3. Lee commits his reserve in the salient, Gordon's division, to counterattack. Besides his own units, Gordon is given Perrin's Brigade from Mahone's division. The counterattack begins around 5.30am and the disorganized Union assault wave is pushed back out of the salient.

4. Wright assaults the west face of the angle with Neill's and Russell's divisions, but is repulsed as routed Confederate units re-form and begin to fight back.

5. Warren attacks Anderson's line east of Old Courthouse Road at 8.15am and again at 10.00am and is repulsed both times. Mahone's division is then drawn off to reinforce actions on the east side of the entrenchments.

6. Heth counterattacks into Burnside's flank at 2.00pm, causing any other action on that front to cease. Heth creates a small salient of his own.

7. To mitigate his losses, Lee has a trench line dug across the base of the salient and pulls his men back to it after dark, shortening his line.

ASSAULT ON THE MULE SHOE SALIENT, 4.30AM, MAY 12, 1864
The attack that almost ended the war.

top they went, diving into the churning masses of surprised Rebels. Bayonets bristled in every direction as the Union men stabbed, clubbed and scattered the enemy. Caught either sleeping or cooking, Johnson's division was unable to resist.

The Rebel artillery already in lunettes were manhandled around and turned on their former owners. Lee's hasty order to return the artillery found most of it limbered. William Carter was just one of the battery commanders caught in the attack. His men managed to unlimber their guns and fire a single volley before being surrounded by Yankees.

The Rebels began to surrender in droves. Allegheny Johnson's men were surrounded and had to give up. Brigades under Colonel William Witcher and George Steuart were gone in minutes. Birney was also having good luck, smashing Colonel Zebulon York's Louisianans and sending the Stonewall Brigade reeling. Over a dozen cannon were taken at that point. More than half a mile of the Mule Shoe was cleared. Half a dozen Confederate brigades were captured or in full retreat. It looked bad for Lee.

Hancock was ecstatic when he sent word to Meade. Over 2,000 Rebels were being marched to the rear along with 20 pieces of artillery, though some were being used by the jubilant Yankee troops. It was a strange time. Heading to the rear were Confederate generals Johnson and Steuart.

Johnson was taken directly to Meade and Grant and he arrived around 6.30am. He was familiar to Meade as a West Point man. Grant knew him from Mexico. The group sat around and had a pleasant conversation before Johnson was led away, eventually to be exchanged for a Union prisoner.

Steuart's ordeal was different. When overrun, "Maryland" Steuart surrendered to Colonel James Beaver of the 148th Pennsylvania. Beaver asked his name, to which the hapless Confederate replied, "General Steuart." Beaver's heart was in his throat: "What? Jeb Stuart?" Steuart shook his head. "No, George H. Steuart of the infantry." Beaver attempted to get Steuart's sword, which was missing and sent the Rebel to Hancock under escort of a lowly corporal.

Hancock recognized Steuart and stuck out his hand. Steuart, grumpy over his capture and ignominious treatment, snarled, "Under the present circumstances, I must decline to take your hand." Hancock's mood darkened immediately: "Under any other circumstances, General, I should not have offered it." Johnson was allowed to ride to the rear on a horse given to him by Hancock, but he made Steuart walk.

Back at the salient, Hancock's regiments were dissolving into a churning mob of bluecoats, continuing to surge forward as Rebel opposition tried to stiffen. After Colonel William Monaghan's brigade was sent packing, Brigadier-General Junius Daniel put his North Carolina men at a 90 degree angle to the works to try to slow Birney's men at the west side of the salient. Seeing the Union men advancing deeper into the salient, the Confederates wheeled and fired into them. The assault was too packed for any shot to miss. Men were falling in clumps as momentum began to slow.

The battle reached its tipping point at 5.30am. John B. Gordon, whose late assault at the Wilderness nearly rolled up the Union line a week previous, was in command of the reserves – his

Edward "Allegheny" Johnson was the highest-ranking commander captured at the battle. His Confederate division effectively ceased to exist the morning of May 12. Some 2,000 were made prisoner. (Library of Congress)

George "Maryland" Steuart led a brigade of Virginians into captivity as the Union overwhelmed his part of the Bloody Angle on May 12. His poor attitude upon capture earned him no respect from his old classmate Winfield Hancock. (Library of Congress)

division, now all three brigades strong. As soon as possible, he sent off Brigadier-General Robert D. Johnston's North Carolina Brigade to try to plug the hole. Johnston's men advanced into the buzzsaw and were thrown back, Johnston himself falling.

Down to two brigades, Gordon put in part of his old Georgians, but they, too, were swallowed up by the blue wave and nearly all captured. Desperate to stop the surge, Gordon formed a line with his remaining troops, the unused Georgians under Colonel Clement Evans and Colonel John Hoffman's (ex-Pegram's) brigade before the Harrison House. Turning, Gordon saw Robert E. Lee on Traveler, riding between the center units of his hasty line.

This photo was taken from the crest of the line towards the Union advance through the tangled underbrush before the Bloody Angle. Silent, Hancock's two divisions made their way through the fog toward the sleeping Confederates at 4am on May 12. (Photo by Rich Allen)

Historians have pondered whether Lee was merely rallying his men as he did with Gregg's Texans in the Wilderness or whether he felt responsible for the debacle at the Mule Shoe, but there he was, hat in hand on his splendid horse. Gordon and staff officers crowded around their commander who listened as Gordon explained his situation. Lee approved and Gordon turned to send the men forward. When he looked back, Lee was still coming forward!

Yankee bullets were increasingly singing about the area as Gordon and several officers formed a line between Lee and the approaching Federals. The thin, bitter Gordon became agitated. "General Lee," he said, "this is no place for you." Shouts of "Lee to the rear" and "We will drive them back, General" grew as the men became aghast at the thought of their hero-general falling in battle. Men wept, hands grabbed at Traveler and finally a Virginia sergeant took the reins and led Lee around.

Incensed, Gordon and his men rose up and rushed forward, firing a ragged volley and screaming at the top of their lungs. They hit the Union line fast and hard. Edgy and exhausted by the hard charge and continual barrage of shot and shell, the men in blue were at the end of their endurance. Gordon's regiments slammed into them, driving them back and expelling most of them through the section formerly occupied by the unfortunate Steuart.

Other Rebel brigades jockeyed to support Gordon. Brigadier-General Stephen Ramseur's brigade, down the west side of the salient, was snatched

This modern photograph shows the location of the McCoull House, which John B. Gordon used as a landmark while forming his counterattack. You can see the Bloody Angle in the far distance. (Author's photograph)

up and thrown alongside Daniel's brigade. Barely holding the line, Ramseur took a bullet to his arm and his brigade was taken over by Colonel Bryan Grimes. Grimes' new command was bolstered by Brigadier-General Abner Perrin's Alabamans, part of Mahone's division. Gordon threw Perrin forward across the bloody field toward McCoull House. Perrin was shot from his horse and died as his brigade took flanking fire from the east angle.

This Waud drawing shows Hancock and Wright conferring behind the Union artillery at 1pm on May 12. Workmen improve the position to the left and the battle of the salient rages in the background. By then, the Union gains had been largely erased. (Library of Congress)

Meade roared at Hancock to keep the attack going, but Hancock's men were too tired and disorganized to do much more than cling to the tip of what was to go down in history as "the Bloody Angle." As the awful carnage continued, other parts of the battlefield were also disappointing Meade and Grant.

THE REST OF MAY 12

Grant got the news of Hancock's coup around 5.30am. Pleased by the initial results, he sent word to Wright to send Brigadier Thomas Neill's 2nd and Brigadier-General James Rickett's 3rd Divisions forward to help storm the works in support of II Corps.

Wright sent them forward, then lurched as a piece of shrapnel sliced into him. The wound was minor and Wright continued to direct his men. Neill's men went in next to Mott's line along the west side of the Angle about a quarter mile down from the tip. Brigadier-General Lewis Grant's brigade peeled off to cover Barlow's division as it came back from the hellish cauldron inside the Angle.

The VI Corps attack ran into the wave of Confederate reinforcements. Both sides fired volley after volley before crashing together. Brigadier-General Nathaniel Harris' brigade hit Mott's division like a thunderbolt, throwing back the Excelsior Brigade and freeing up some of Ramseur's men to enfilade Mott, sending more Federals back toward their entrenchments. Into this melee waded Brigadier-General Samuel McGowan's brigade of South Carolinians from Wilcox's division. McGowan went down and so did the second in command and three other colonels or lieutenant-colonels. Finally, Lieutenant-Colonel Isaac Hunt of the 13th South Carolina led the remnant into line by Harris and the Yankees fell back but both sides fired at each other for the rest of the day.

Thure de Thulstrup did this amazing painting of the fight for the Bloody Angle for the L. Prang Company in 1887. It shows the Union soldiers from II Corps spilling over the Confederate breastworks, going to work with bayonet and rifle butt as the sleepy defenders struggle to hold the line. (Library of Congress)

Instead of Ricketts, Wright unleashed Russell's 1st Division with Emory Upton leading the way to take pressure off Neill's right flank. The Rebels greeted them with a hail of bullets, dozens of men going down as they scrambled up the slope of the west Angle. Upton's voice rang above the din: "Hold this ground!" Suddenly, the clouds shook forth an awful rainstorm. Upton persisted, upsetting several more experienced commanders who considered him as an outsider as he tried to move their troops up the deadly slopes.

The Confederate firepower rippling down from above was devastating. Whole regiments were shattered and no gains could be made. Those units lucky enough to gain the entrenchments were soon thrown back. Upton tried to move up a section of artillery, but the guns were abandoned as most of the crew, some 23 out of 24, were either killed or wounded. More guns came up and now both sides were sending murderous volleys at each other.

The Confederates were taking awful casualties as well, drawing men from quieter sectors. The afternoon wore on with more bodies piling up. One assault never got through the remnants of McGowan's brigade, but was hurled back in a savage melee of rifle butts and bayonets. Colonel Oliver Edwards tried to pull back in order for his men to rest at 4pm only to have them ordered back in line at 6pm, causing Edwards to become so angry he pulled a pistol on an officer from II Corps who tried to interfere.

Men in the rear ranks reloaded muskets and handed them forward in continuous rotation as men in the front stood on the works firing into the trenches then passed their weapon back. Others threw large items like fence rails over the rim to try to incapacitate defenders. The Confederates had no time to reload and used their bayonets whenever an enemy appeared.

Trees, fences, even the grass was stripped bare by the unceasing gunfire. Blood mixed with rain and ran down the slopes. Wounded rarely survived close to the works as random bullets slammed into still forms. The Confederates stacked their dead outside their trenches to get them out of the lines.

Any relief would have to come from either Burnside's IX Corps or Warren's V Corps, since neither side could or would disengage from the Bloody Angle. Burnside sent Brigadier-General Robert Potter's 2nd Division forward at 4am, followed by Brigadier-General Daniel Crittenden's 1st Division. They advanced over some largely abandoned entrenchments, picking up the odd prisoner as they tried to maintain contact with Hancock's glorious assault.

Soon, though, Potter's men found stiff opposition and had to back off from the volume of fire. The line held, but the advance stopped as the Yankees dug in. Seeing Hancock's left still ragged at 5.45am, Grant urged Burnside on, reporting Hancock's stunning breakthrough. Seeing no movement, Grant tried again at 8am and 10.30am, but Burnside was in no hurry to sacrifice his men, mindful of the slaughter he led at Fredericksburg. After Grant's last command, Burnside shuffled Brigadier-General Orlando Willcox's 3rd Division to form the link with II Corps.

Burnside changed his mind and ordered Willcox to move around Crittenden so he could attack to the left of 1st Division by 2pm. Coincidentally, Confederate Henry Heth's and Cadmus Wilcox's divisions were angled to smash

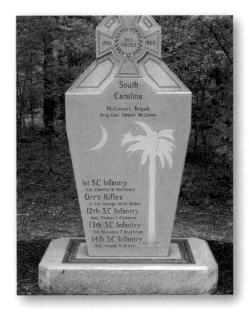

This monument marks the part of the line that Confederate Brigadier-General Samuel McGowan and his South Carolina Brigade held their part of the salient. (Author's photograph)

UNION SUCCESS AT THE BLOODY ANGLE, 4.30AM, MAY 12, 1864 (PP. 82–83)

Union Maj. Gen. Winfield Hancock had been instructed to have his men move up under the cover of fog and drizzle to assault a portion of the Confederate lines known as the Mule Shoe salient. If manned and alert, the bulging salient would be impregnable, but using the woods and bad weather as cover, Hancock assembled three divisions of his corps and left a fourth in reserve. Starting from Brown House, his men rushed through the dense fog as the rain tapered off. In front of the Confederate lines were cut-down trees whose branches had been sharpened to impale would-be attackers. Special teams went ahead and pushed them away or chopped them apart **(1)**.

Hancock's surprise was complete. The Confederates, exhausted from the previous day were mostly asleep. The main attack fell on the division of Confederate Maj. Gen. Edward Johnson from Ewell's Corps. Union soldiers clambered up the piles of earth in front of the wooden walls of the entrenchments, firing down into the hapless defenders as they struggled to resist. **(2)** Union

soldiers, unable to reload, threw anything they could down into the trenches to disable defenders, even fence rails **(3)**. Once the defenders had been thrown back from the trenches, the Union soldiers leaped among the dazed enemy, employing the bayonet to deadly effect. **(4)** Johnson was captured, along with one of his brigade commanders, Brig. Gen. George "Maryland" Steuart, who was taken before he could buckle on his sword. **(5)**

Hancock's men captured over 2,000 of Johnson's division, along with a number of cannon, and for the next hour routed regiment after regiment, leaving the victorious soldiers in blue tired and disorganized. They were counterattacked by John B. Gordon's division and their success ended in an ignominious retreat back across the bloody ground they conquered only an hour before. The savage fighting gave that part of the Confederate entrenchments the sobriquet the Bloody Angle. Today it is a pleasant rolling meadow, with only a sign to note the violence of 150 years past.

Burnside's flank. Burnside's waffling left his left flank flapping in the air. Brigadier-General James Lane, a veteran of Pickett's charge at Gettysburg, led his brigade from Wilcox and Colonel David Weisiger, leading Mahone's brigade, jumped at the opportunity.

They tried to take out the Union artillery, but only managed to suppress it until infantry could be brought up. Willcox's men were in motion as the Confederate attack developed and were quickly sent packing. Burnside's men dug in and managed to limit follow-up attacks.

Warren, on the western side of the salient, was ordered to attack at 6am. At 7.30am, Meade tried to get Warren to support Wright, who was having trouble supporting Hancock. Warren released Brigadier-General Joseph Bartlett's brigade and Colonel J. Howard Kitching's gunners from the Heavy Artillery Brigade.

Unsatisfied, Grant leaned on Meade, who leaned on Warren to attack with whatever he could spare. Warren fumbled around a bit, complaining about a curve in the enemy line that was able to enfilade his position, pointing out in a series of replies to Meade that this made it impossible to attack until VI Corps had successfully assaulted the works and eliminated the threat to his left flank.

Meade's temper flared and he ordered Warren to attack at 9.15am regardless of position and do so with all troops. Calming a bit, Meade clarified his earlier demand, acceding to Warren's earlier request for Bartlett's brigade to return to V Corps and trying to convince him that Hancock and Wright were drawing in a huge number of enemy troops, so Warren should face lighter opposition. He even signed one note "your friend."

Dolefully, Warren bowed to Meade's wishes, trepidation evident in his reply to Meade. Griffin's and Cutler's divisions moved out over the rolling field and were stopped cold by a blast of muskets from Colonel John Bratton's and Colonel Dudley Dubose's brigades. The Iron Brigade from Cutler's division, with two more brigades behind them, rushed forward. They got to the crest of the emplacements only to be knocked back by a storm of Minié balls and canister.

The right end of Warren's line advanced tenderly, many having enlistments ready to expire, and so did little to cause the Confederates alarm. Warren gave up at 10.30am, making no headway. Grant was so upset he complained openly to his staff at his disappointment with Warren, for whom he previously had so much respect. There was serious talk of relieving him.

Meade left Warren in place, but his attack was done for the day. He maintained his position. The two divisions that had suffered earlier, Griffin's and Cutler's, went to support Hancock and Wright. Only Crawford remained in place to hold the line.

Lee took advantage of Warren's half-hearted attempt and re-arranged his line. Realizing that the Mule Shoe was too exposed, he ordered a line dug across the base of the salient, using non-attached men and filled by pulling Brigadier-General Benjamin Humphrey's and John Bratton's brigades out of line. The Confederate commander's doubts about his ability to maintain his bulging salient were not shared by the men, who felt increasingly confident as the day wore on.

The fear that the Rebels might suddenly counterattack caused Grant's corps commanders to become cautious as their losses mounted. Such fears eventually reached Grant, who reluctantly felt it was no use to try another assault and made no plans for a renewed attack the next day. Darkness fell on two weary armies, and night weighed the heaviest on Grant, whose day started with such promise but ended with his commanders unable or unwilling to try again.

The battle of Spotsylvania, May 13–19

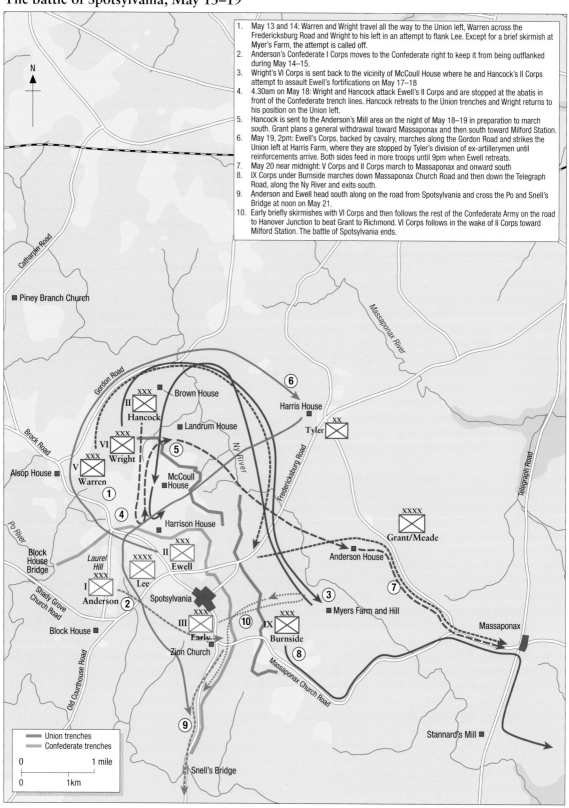

1. May 13 and 14: Warren and Wright travel all the way to the Union left, Warren across the Fredericksburg Road and Wright to his left in an attempt to flank Lee. Except for a brief skirmish at Myer's Farm, the attempt is called off.
2. Anderson's Confederate I Corps moves to the Confederate right to keep it from being outflanked during May 14–15.
3. Wright's VI Corps is sent back to the vicinity of McCoull House where he and Hancock's II Corps attempt to assault Ewell's fortifications on May 17–18
4. 4.30am on May 18: Wright and Hancock attack Ewell's II Corps and are stopped at the abatis in front of the Confederate trench lines. Hancock retreats to the Union trenches and Wright returns to his position on the Union left.
5. Hancock is sent to the Anderson's Mill area on the night of May 18–19 in preparation to march south. Grant plans a general withdrawal toward Massaponax and then south toward Milford Station.
6. May 19, 2pm: Ewell's Corps, backed by cavalry, marches along the Gordon Road and strikes the Union left at Harris Farm, where they are stopped by Tyler's division of ex-artillerymen until reinforcements arrive. Both sides feed in more troops until 9pm when Ewell retreats.
7. May 20 near midnight: V Corps and II Corps march to Massaponax and onward south
8. IX Corps under Burnside marches down Massaponax Church Road and then down the Telegraph Road, along the Ny River and exits south.
9. Anderson and Ewell head south along on the road from Spotsylvania and cross the Po and Snell's Bridge at noon on May 21.
10. Early briefly skirmishes with VI Corps and then follows the rest of the Confederate Army on the road to Hanover Junction to beat Grant to Richmond. VI Corps follows in the wake of II Corps toward Milford Station. The battle of Spotsylvania ends.

AFTERMATH

The next day was gray and sullen, rain sluicing away blood from the churned ground. The exhausted living lay as still as the dead, heedless of the muddy ground or soaking showers. Their respite was short. Lee pulled his men back from the Mule Shoe to his newly prepared line.

Union troops advanced cautiously as II and VI Corps tried to maintain contact with the enemy. Hopes that Lee was withdrawing were smashed as V Corps found the enemy still entrenched before them. Other than some skirmishing, little action took place that day. Over 10,000 casualties littered the field, the majority dressed in blue. Lee's casualties, though, included the 2,000 or so prisoners from Johnson's division.

Both sides lost key officers and burial parties worked to exhaustion amid the piteous cries of the wounded. The dead were found in various positions, many hit numerous times. They were stretched out and buried in rows. Some in the trenches were buried in their emplacements.

While the men toiled or slept, Grant planned his next move. Instead of a general attack, Grant conceived a plan to load up the left of his line with all four corps in a swift march and try to overwhelm Lee's right flank.

Grant set Wright and Warren in motion to move below Burnside and assault across the Ny at 4am on the 14th. He gave orders for the two corps to begin moving at 8pm on the 13th and everything went wrong from there.

Warren had trouble getting started and it was closer to 10pm by the time his corps took the road. They immediately encountered rivers of mud rather than roads and bogged down immediately. The line became strung out as the tired, wet men became exhausted, slowing or stopping as their mud-caked shoes turned to cold, heavy blocks. There was no way the two corps could get in position with enough force and so the attack was called off.

The only notable action was a confused battle for a rise of land called Myer's Hill. Occupying the hill was Upton and 800 men. He asked for help and got two regiments, but two brigades were hitting him. Worse, Meade arrived to look at the enemy's position from the hill. The rested Rebels drove Upton from the hill, putting Meade into an angry flight.

Dead soldiers and scattered fence rails mark the spot where Ewell attempted to strike back at the Union line on May 19. He failed through lack of mass, not determination. (Library of Congress)

Thomas Rosser and his cavalry brigade tried to smash through the Union line of mostly green soldiers, but a veteran Maryland unit helped keep them from making a breakthrough. (University of Kentucky)

After Ewell's attack sputtered out, wounded were brought to nearby Alsop House for care. (Library of Congress)

He demanded the hill be retaken but his attacking force found that the enemy vacated the area rather than face overwhelming odds.

Meade's surprise reverse caused him to order Hancock to march around IX, V, and VI Corps, to land on Warren's left, leaving Birney's division to guard IX Corps' left. Lee, for his part, shifted men around to meet the new Union position, but did little to respond.

Grant decided to wait for fresh troops, so his commanders dug in. The War Department scraped out troops from the Washington, DC, area and swelled Grant's numbers beyond his starting size. Most were untried troops, and a brigade of Irish troops from New York was suspected of drunkenness. Both sides settled down, anticipating a renewal at any moment.

Grant waited as long as his disposition would allow. He next considered a strike at the Confederate left, so he set his army in motion for one more thrust, this time to strike the line at the base of the Mule Shoe. He relayed his decision to Meade, who in turn ordered II Corps to march at 7pm on the 17th to the general area around Landrum House, with Wright leapfrogging II Corps and striking toward Harrison House.

The attack was to start at 4am on the 18th. Wright ran late and a new II Corps division had some problems getting into position, but Hancock attacked at 4.30am. His men found the Rebel trenches full of defenders and 24 cannon, ready to sweep the field before the emplacements.

Hancock's men surged forward across a plain covered with rotting corpses, sickening the men and impeding progress. The attack was stopped cold as men were tangled up in a dense abatis ring. Grant received the news with ill humor, his mood further dampened by reports that Generals Ben Butler's and Franz Sigel's maneuvers were stymied as well.

Tired of bashing his head against a brick wall, Grant decided it was time to maneuver again. He thought about cutting Hancock loose and trying to get him between Lee and Richmond, forcing the Confederate general out of his fortifications and allowing Grant to catch up and pile on Lee while the latter maneuvered to crush Hancock. To help lighten his army, Grant sent 100 cannon off to Washington.

The idea was appealing, anything to get the army out of the unhealthy charnel house it currently occupied. He ordered Hancock to begin moving early on May 20 in the general direction of Milford Station. While Grant planned to dangle Hancock before Lee, Lee was ready to hit back.

His nature kept worrying him to find a place to hit the Union and force a

retreat. Thinking the Federal right flank weak since Grant shuffled his units around, Lee ordered Ewell to leave his trenches and try to outflank Grant. Ewell was ready to attack, sending Rodes' and Gordon's crack divisions across the Ny along with Rosser's cavalry brigade.

Taking a wide path toward Alsop and then right, 6,000 infantry marched out a bit after 2pm on May 19. This part of Grant's line was held by the converted gunners from several heavy artillery brigades (1st Maine, 2nd New York and 8th New York Heavy Artillery), green men all, though they had the veteran 1st Maryland, just back from furlough, to stiffen them. Around 4.30pm, the Rebels fell on them and began to give them a thrashing.

The problem with Ewell's attack was lack of numbers. As his assault threw back the artillerymen, more Union troops came forward, extending Ewell's line and thinning his mass. The attack slowed, then stopped shy of the Fredericksburg Road. Tossing in the veteran 1st Maryland Brigade and Pennsylvania Reserve Division, the Yankees were able to extend their line far enough to flank Gordon.

At 5.30pm Meade ordered Hancock to send his men forward to support the green troops who bent but did not break. Lee tried to stop the Union move north by sending Early out to hit Warren, but to no avail. Wade Hampton, with Rosser, returned and hit the Union rear, causing enough grief to allow Ewell to withdraw, but not before he was thrown to the ground after his horse was killed. The dark covered the Confederate retreat, leaving 900 men for no result, except 1,500 Union casualties from an army that could better afford them.

Ewell's attack did cost Grant some time, however. He hesitated long enough to see if Lee was planning on outflanking him and falling on the supply train at Fredericksburg. Once satisfied the supplies were safe, he put Hancock in motion behind Torbert's Cavalry Division on the road to Milford Station. Warren was to move next, crossing the Po along Telegraph Road, followed by IX Corps while Wright would fall in behind II Corps.

Hancock started at 11pm on the 19th. He was delayed and Warren was rerouted toward Guinea Station. Lee figured out Grant's plan after some judicious probing. He was prepared to continue the fight with reinforcements trickling in from more successful fronts near Richmond and the Shenandoah Valley, swelling his ranks by nearly 10,000 men. Even A. P. Hill was back, feeling better.

All to no avail. As at the Wilderness, Grant was slipping around Lee's flank and the Confederate commander had to scramble to put his army between Grant and Richmond. He set Ewell and Anderson on the road to Hanover Junction, leaving Hill to guard a deserted battlefield until dark, when he left the corpse-strewn entrenchments. The two would meet again at the North Anna River, but for the time being, the battle was over.

A dead Rebel at the Bloody Angle, likely posed by the photographer, is mute testimony to the violent struggle that left him and many more strewn along the miles of Virginia woodland during the first 19 days of May, 1864. Note the "bull's-eye" canteen and slouch hat popular with Confederate troops. (Library of Congress)

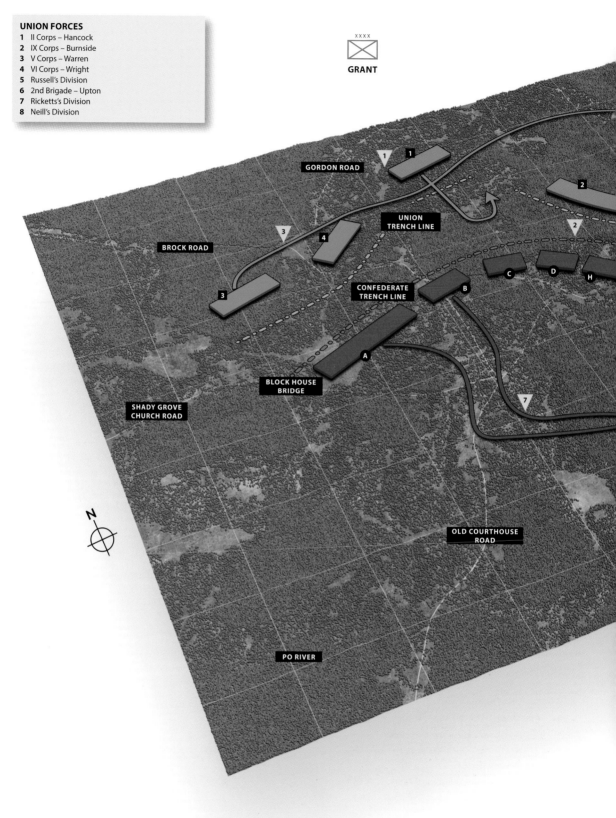

UNION FORCES
1 II Corps – Hancock
2 IX Corps – Burnside
3 V Corps – Warren
4 VI Corps – Wright
5 Russell's Division
6 2nd Brigade – Upton
7 Ricketts's Division
8 Neill's Division

GRANT

GORDON ROAD

UNION
TRENCH LINE

BROCK ROAD

CONFEDERATE
TRENCH LINE

BLOCK HOUSE
BRIDGE

SHADY GROVE
CHURCH ROAD

OLD COURTHOUSE
ROAD

N

PO RIVER

Note: Gridlines are shown at intervals of 1km

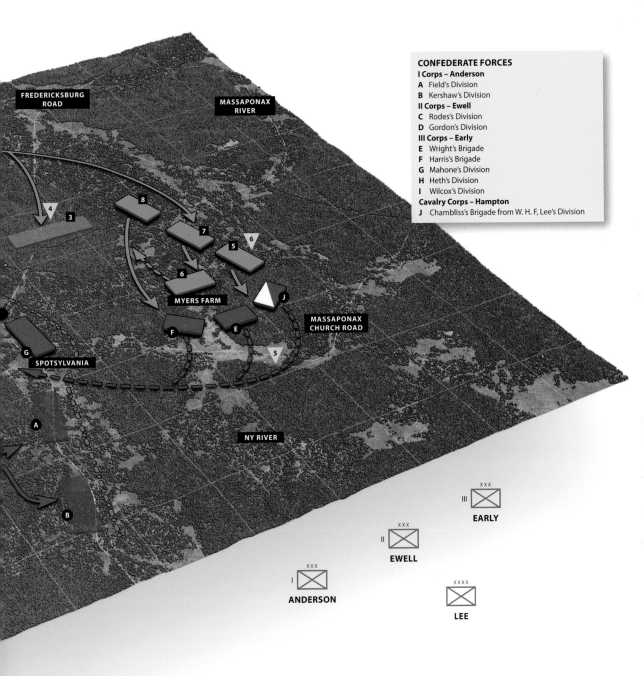

CONFEDERATE FORCES

I Corps – Anderson
A Field's Division
B Kershaw's Division
II Corps – Ewell
C Rodes's Division
D Gordon's Division
III Corps – Early
E Wright's Brigade
F Harris's Brigade
G Mahone's Division
H Heth's Division
I Wilcox's Division
Cavalry Corps – Hampton
J Chambliss's Brigade from W. H. F, Lee's Division

FREDERICKSBURG ROAD

MASSAPONAX RIVER

MYERS FARM

MASSAPONAX CHURCH ROAD

SPOTSYLVANIA

NY RIVER

III ⊠ xxx **EARLY**

II ⊠ xxx **EWELL**

I ⊠ xxx **ANDERSON**

⊠ xxxx **LEE**

EVENTS

1. May 13, 3.00am: the Confederates withdraw from the Mule Shoe to their new line below Harrison House. At 5.30am units from Union VI and II Corps advance into the salient.

2. 7.30am: skirmishing starts as the Union units close on the new Confederate line. After suffering casualties including a brigade commander, the Union troops withdraw to the original Confederate trenches.

3. Grant orders V and VI Corps to swing around to the Union left near the Fredericksburg Road and attack at 4.00am. Warren moves out at 10:00pm.

4. Warren arrives across the Ny with less than 4,000 men available for combat due to muddy road conditions. Grant calls off the attack at 9.00am on the 14th.

5. Wright takes a slightly different route that puts him to the left of Warren around 9.00am. He sends Upton's brigade to occupy a hill containing the Myers' Farm. Upton's four regiments relieve an advance force which earlier repulsed Chambliss' brigade. Feeling his 800-man brigade inadequate, Upton requests reinforcements and is sent two New Jersey regiments from Brown's 1st Brigade. Meade arrives after noon. Around 4.00pm, two Confederate brigades from Mahone's division advance on the hill. Chambliss' brigade returns and fires upon Upton's left flank. Unable to withstand the assault, Upton withdraws and Meade barely escapes with his life.

6. Determined to retake the position, Meade orders Wright to assault the hill. He puts Russell on the left and Ricketts on the right, leaving Neill in reserve near Anderson house. He advances only to find that the Confederates have withdrawn.

7. Lee, cognizant of this threat to his right flank, orders Anderson to march to the Old Courthouse Road and put a line of entrenchments along it to join up with Early sometime around 3.30pm. The day ends with no advantage to either side.

THE ACTION OF MAY 14, 1864
Meade scrambles and Upton gets his comeuppance.

THE BATTLEFIELDS TODAY

Fredericksburg and Spotsylvania National Military Park was established on February 14, 1927 by the War Department and later turned over to the National Park Service. The Park encompasses four Civil War battlefields: Fredericksburg, Chancellorsville, the Wilderness and Spotsylvania. According to Park information, it stretches some 17 miles and covers an area where 100,000 men became casualties during the Civil War. Today, the Wilderness Battlefield is still lush and green, but the terrain has changed somewhat to include three man-made lakes, draining some of the marshiness that soldiers encountered in the battle. Instead of fords, highways now cross the Rapidan where Grant began his campaign. From Fredericksburg, the visitor takes Route 3 then left on Route 20 where an Exhibit Shelter is located near Gordon's flank attack.

On one of the occasions I visited the Park, I took a walking tour of Gordon's flank attack. You can appreciate the density of the Wilderness as you take the trail around Sedgwick's flank, where trench lines, now softened by time, still show the area where the tide of battle nearly turned.

A visit to the intersection of Brock Road and Orange Plank Road gives the visitor a sense of how confused the battle became in the thick woods where fire and smoke caused Longstreet to be shot by his own men. Trails marked by signs meander through the heavy woods, and you get a sense of the enormity of the battlefield. I walked Tapp Field and stood where Lee was caught up by the arrival of Gregg's Texans, shouting with glee as they went to their deaths to stem Hancock's assault on May 6. A few housing developments mar the pristine landscape, but they are tucked away in the green vastness of the Wilderness.

Recently, the battlefield was threatened by the possibility of having part of it sloughed off for a ubiquitous Wal-Mart, but popular outcry has defeated the idea for now. From Route 20, you can take Hill-Ewell Drive and circle along the main battle lines, then to the intersection of Orange Plank Road, Route 621. Taking a left there will get you to the Brock Road, Route 613 intersection, and a right turn there puts you on your way to Spotsylvania. Along the way you pass the site of Todd's Tavern.

After a dozen miles or so, the visitor arrives at the Spotsylvania Battlefield Exhibit Shelter, not far from Laurel Hill, near the junction of Route 648. From there, visitors can ride along three roads that follow the entrenchments. The land is pleasant and rolling through here, less wooded than the Wilderness. Along the entrenchments are winding roads and grassy fields. Near the Exhibit Shelter is the start of a rubberized path that winds along the parapets of the Bloody Angle. Dotting the landscape are monuments to units on both sides that participated in the battle, along with interpretive signboards.

You can stand, as the author did, along the Angle and look down into the woods at the incline Hancock's troops scrambled up to catch the Confederates unawares, and see across the rippling plain to gauge the size of the assault. I ran into a fellow there who disabused me of my assumption of where the initial breakthrough occurred, and showed me where the semi-circular patterns of artillery lunettes still appeared in the greenery covering the battlefield. A short distance along Gordon Drive takes visitors to the site of McCoull House, where Gordon saved the day for the Confederates after they were driven from the Mule Shoe salient.

The encroachment of American suburbia has hemmed in other areas, and major roads now span the Ny River where Burnside tried to drive in the Confederate flank between the Ny and the Po Rivers. Though 15,000 Union soldiers are buried in Fredericksburg atop Marye's Heights from all battles in the area, you can find the Confederate cemetery near the Spotsylvania County Museum along Courthouse Road (Route 208). Park literature advises that 85 percent of all the interred are unknown.

In fact, the entire battlefield area looks so peaceful and bucolic that markers, signboards and road names fail to give the visitor a sense of the violent, desperate battle that swirled all around them as they tour the battlefield. Torn, muddy earth where combatants screamed out their final breaths have been replaced by a pastoral stillness; the only sounds coming from bird or insect, save for the occasional vehicle full of people trying to get a sense of history from the beauty around them.

FURTHER READING

Battles and Leaders of the Civil War, Volume 4, New York (undated)

Alexander, Edward Porter, *Fighting for the Confederacy*, Chapel Hill, 1989

Cleaves, Freeman, *Meade of Gettysburg*, Dayton, 1980

Commager, Henry Steele, *The Blue and the Gray, Volume 2*, New York, 1950

Cannan, John, *The Wilderness Campaign*, Conshohocken, 1993

——, *The Spotsylvania Campaign*, Conshohocken, 1997

Davis, William C., ed., *The Confederate General (6 volumes)*, 1991

Freeman, Douglas Southall, *Lee's Lieutenants (3 volumes)*, New York, 1970

——, *R. E. Lee, A Biography (4 volumes)*, New York, 1977

Gallagher, Gary, ed., *The Wilderness Campaign*, Chapel Hill, 1997

Longstreet, James, *From Manassas to Appomattox*, Secaucus, 1988

Marvel, William, *Burnside*, Chapel Hill, 1991

Matter, William, *If It Takes All Summer: The Battle of Spotsylvania*, Chapel Hill, 1988

McFeely, William S., *Grant, A Biography*, New York, 1981

McWhiney, Grady, *Battle in the Wilderness*, Fort Worth, 1995

Newton, Steven H., *Lost for the Cause: The Confederate Army in 1864*, Mason City, 2000

Pfanz, Donald C., *Richard S. Ewell: A Soldier's Life*, Chapel Hill, 1998

Rhea, Gordon C., *The Battle of the Wilderness*, Baton Rouge, 1994

——, *The Battles for Spotsylvania Courthouse and the Road to Yellow Tavern*, Baton Rouge, 1997

Robertson, James I., Jr., *General A. P. Hill: The Story of a Confederate Warrior*, New York, 1987

Sifakis, Stewart, *Who Was Who in the Civil War*, New York, 1988

Steere, Edward, *The Wilderness Campaign*, Harrisburg, 1960

Thomas, Emory M., *Bold Dragoon: The Life of J. E. B. Stuart*, New York, 1988

Trudeau, Noah Andre, *Bloody Roads South*, Boston, 1989

Wert, Jeffrey D., *General James Longstreet*, New York, 1993

INDEX